MW00353869

MAN vs FISH

At home on the Rio

MAN vs FISH

The Fly Fisherman's Eternal Struggle

Text and Photographs by

TAYLOR STREIT

Foreword by JOHN NICHOLS

University of New Mexico Press

Albuquerque

© 2007 by Taylor Streit

All rights reserved. Published 2007

Printed in Singapore by Tien Wah Press

12 11 10 09 08 07   1 2 3 4 5 6 7

Library of Congress Cataloging-in-Publication Data

Streit, Taylor.
Man vs fish : the fly fisherman's eternal struggle /
          Taylor Streit ; foreword by John Nichols.
          p. cm.
          ISBN 978-0-8263-3272-1 (cloth : alk. paper)
1. Fly fishing—Anecdotes. 2. Streit, Taylor. 1. Title.
 SH456.S844 2007
 799.12'4—dc22
                          2007010398

DESIGN AND COMPOSITION: Mina Yamashita

CONTENTS

Foreword by John Nichols / vii

Acknowledgments / xiii

PART I: NEW MEXICO
CHAPTER ONE: Rivers of the North / 1

CHAPTER TWO: Ole Walter / 5

CHAPTER THREE: Egocentricity / 12

CHAPTER FOUR: Red River Blues / 20

CHAPTER FIVE: My Valle Vidal / 26

PART II: RIO GRANDE
CHAPTER SIX: Fishing with Nichols / 31

CHAPTER SEVEN: Colleen / 38

CHAPTER EIGHT: The Side Less Fished / 42

PART III: SOUTH AMERICA
CHAPTER NINE: Amazon / 49

CHAPTER TEN: The Five-Peso Float—Part I / 58

CHAPTER ELEVEN: The Five-Peso Float—Part II / 62

CHAPTER TWELVE: By Hook or by Crook / 68

CHAPTER THIRTEEN: Argentine Lakes / 71

CHAPTER FOURTEEN: The Royal Brookie / 73

CHAPTER FIFTEEN: Crying for the Argentine / 82

CHAPTER SIXTEEN: Adrift in Patagonia / 87

PART IV: SALT WATER

CHAPTER SEVENTEEN: Man's Superiority to Fish / 95

CHAPTER EIGHTEEN: Blue Hole Snapper / 99

CHAPTER NINETEEN: Marlin / 109

PART V: HUNTING

CHAPTER TWENTY: Life and Death on the Sierra Alto / 117

CHAPTER TWENTY-ONE: Raising an Elk Hunter / 123

CHAPTER TWENTY-TWO: Zeus—God of Bird Dogs / 129

CHAPTER TWENTY-THREE: FIFTY / 135

PART VI: COLLATERAL DAMAGE

CHAPTER TWENTY-FOUR: Animals / 141

CHAPTER TWENTY-FIVE: Humans / 146

CHAPTER TWENTY-SIX: Big for Its Size / 150

CHAPTER TWENTY-SEVEN: Ice Fishin' at Eagle Nest / 153

PART VII: WHICH WAY'S UPSTREAM?

CHAPTER TWENTY-EIGHT: The Legend of Super Fly / 157

CHAPTER TWENTY-NINE: Super Fly Sighting—by Warren Dean McClenagan / 161

CHAPTER THIRTY: The Legend of Spifmeister / 170

Foreword

John Nichols

■ ■ ■

I've known Taylor Streit ever since Moby Dick was a cetacean calf. We both arrived in Taos, New Mexico, around the same time. That would be at the end of the 1960s. The difference between Taylor and me, way back then, was that he could fish and I couldn't. Another difference was that I could write and he couldn't. Unfortunately, I was at the first of many lows in my career, but even then I could make more money writing than Taylor could make fishing.

So at some point I guess Taylor figured that being a writer might be an easier way to earn a buck. Maybe. Yet knowing how to fish and knowing how to write are very different conundrums. To catch fish, all you have to do is tie on a couple of gold-ribbed hare's ears and drop them in a river. Bingo! What could be easier? You're home free, as they say. Basically, fish are stupid.

But to write you have to train for years in Siberian salt mines breaking rock eighteen hours a day with your bare hands. Then you must sit down at a typewriter, hook up an IV of black coffee, and "open a vein," as the famous sports columnist Red Smith once observed.

Compared to fishing, writing is like climbing Mount Everest locked in a straightjacket and shackles. Not many people know how to fish well and write well at the same time. The reason for this is obvious: Anybody in his right mind who knows how to fish would never destroy that joyous avocation by trying to write about it. Writing takes the fun out of everything. Writing is difficult.

I can only think of a few people who've managed to ace both the fishing and writing métiers, and they have names like Ray Bergman, Izaak Walton, Norman Mclean, and Ernest Hemingway.

But now there's Taylor Streit.

Yet in the old days Taylor didn't know the difference between an adverb and a Dolly Parton. I mean a Dolly Varden. In fact, when I first met Taylor, he reminded me of one of those old-fashioned down-and-out gumshoes that used to be played in the movies by Humphrey Bogart or Robert Mitchum. You know the type: three-day stubble, big bags under their sad eyes, heads wreathed in cigarette smoke, large holes in the soles of their brogans. And they always wore a battered fedora so stained by sweat it stunk.

So at first, frankly, I wasn't even sure if Taylor could fish. But I learned pretty quickly that my friend was the Columbo of Taos angling pursuits. He had the raincoat, the cigar, the battered fedora—he was the klutz who always got his man. Or in this case, his fish. And he could teach others to do the same at the drop of a fedora.

Still, I would not have pegged him for a scrivener.

However, miracles happen. Years passed, and I bet Taylor spent every one of those years lying awake at night thinking: I'm stuck in a rut, tying flies and guiding difficult people on difficult rivers—there must be more to life than this. I can't even buy gas for my Rolls, I'm two months behind on the rent, and my divorce lawyer just went south because I couldn't pay his exorbitant tab.

Obviously, it was time for a regime change.

Which is always much easier said than done. Ask George Bush.

I remember some of Taylor's first published stories. In my career I drummed those stories out of my system when I was about sixteen. Taylor got them out of his system when he was forty-five. Still, the man had chutzpah. He was like a guy who wanted to learn a foreign language and was not afraid to speak it. Screw the grammar; forget split infinitives; dispense with past tenses. And don't even think about the subjunctive.

But the lad had heart.

And Taylor parlayed that heart into his first book at age forty-eight. That surprised me. It's a great book called *Fly Fishing New Mexico*. The tome is informative. It moves as fast as an eight-inch brown trout zipping across a shallow pool in a tiny stream toward a Little Joe's hopper being fished dry. Taylor also projects a folksy sense of humor. And there is no bullhockey. He knows what he's talking about, period.

I do have one cavil. On page 17 of Taylor's first book the word "lightning" is mis-spelled three times in one paragraph: "lightening!" Yet Taylor can lure forty trout from the Rio Grande to every one that I bamboozle, so why harp on irrelevant details? They say Scott Fitzgerald couldn't spell worth a damn either.

For a while, watching this man write was like watching Steven Hawking play basketball. No matter; after *Fly Fishing New Mexico* was published, Taylor's stories began to appear in a local newspaper. Admittedly, the early stories were a trifle clumsy. Then they became better. Pretty soon Taylor could use words as expertly as he could use a fly rod, and things changed.

Charles Darwin, take note: evolution works.

Taylor next published a book called *Instinctive Fly Fishing: A Guide's Guide to Better Fishing* in 2003. I blurbed the book because I really liked it. Here's what I said:

> Move over Ray Bergman, Charley Brooks, John Gierach, here comes Taylor Streit upriver waggling his literary fly rod with the best of them in a wonderful, easygoing, and easy-reading book that is sure to find an honored place among the classics. Streit sidesteps the hooky-mooky, he circles dexterously around the convoluted, and he catches the reader constantly with the effortless flick of his magic prose. This is fly-fishing as it should be: simple, direct, humorous, and always right on the money. *Instinctive Fly Fishing* takes out all the stress, leaving behind pure pleasure. Anybody who reads this book can't fail to discover joy on any river . . . and catch plenty of fish to boot.

Overnight, my friend Taylor had become a first-class scribbler. A multifaceted Renaissance man. Not only could he catch 'em, but now he could describe the process as well as anybody else in the genre.

That brings me to the present collection of stories. I read most of them when they were first published, many in the Taos *Horse Fly*, a monthly blat run by a guy named Bill Whaley, who has survived in Taos even longer than Taylor and I have. For several years, whenever *Horse Fly* hit the stands I read Taylor first, that's how much I enjoyed his writing. It was easygoing, fun, funny, informative—in short, well written.

Today, it gives me great pleasure to see many of those stories rubbing elbows in this collection. Taylor has been to exotic places I'll never visit, and he has written about those places. He's caught peacock bass in Brazil. And he has witnessed people wrestling alligators. He bagged a twenty-eight-inch brown trout in Patagonia while red stags kibitzed from the background. Taylor has snagged Bahamian bonefish. He also went after big game in Hawaii, where he landed a "small" marlin that he describes as "only" ten feet long and weighing but "361 pounds."

Yet his agility with words makes that marlin seem much larger and more spectacular than the minnow he actually boated.

Taylor's hunting stories are exciting, sometimes scary. When he gets lost on a deer hunt in terrible weather you are genuinely perturbed. His reveries while stalking quail on a mesa are touching. And Zeus, his incredible bird dog, is a hoot—Zeus being the only canine I ever heard of who could arrive home at night both blasted by a skunk and with a snoot full of porcupine quills.

The best riff in this book is Taylor's story of fishing with me, John Nichols, on the Rio Grande near Taos. Aside from the compelling subject matter, the reason it's the best story is that I, John Nichols, corrected all the grammatical mistakes, reshaped some of the sentences, and offered suggestions for more luminous metaphors. To Taylor's credit, he listened carefully to my suggestions and made judicious changes. Only the great artists can accept criticism and profit from it.

All these stories are fun to read. "The Side Less Fished" makes me laugh because it is so true—a lovely description of a day on the river . . . and in the life of a man.

Taylor says he has heard fishing described as "an endless series of opportunities for hope."

I'd say these stories are an endless series of opportunities for hope.

I remember the essay about Ole Walter from when it first came out. According to Taylor, Ole Walter, a brown trout blind in one eye, measured twenty-six and three-quarter inches. It required years to catch him. And you know a fisherman has made the transition from bullshit artist to fine writer when he or she can resist the temptation to round out that three-quarter inch and make Ole Walter twenty-seven inches even!

Frankly, I don't know if even I could have resisted a temptation like that.

All the tales are good fun and great writing. There's some wonderful satire to boot. Also a hilarious account of ice fishing at Eagle Nest Lake east of Taos that had me gasping at the end. It is so wacky it's believable.

In order to pen this introduction I'm reading an uncorrected manuscript in which the word "lightning" is misspelled as "lightening" God knows how many times. I lost count when I stopped to pour out more bourbon. But I hope the copyeditors will leave that misspelling alone. I am told the Navajos always weave a flaw into their rugs for "the soul to breathe." I think the oft-repeated "lightening" should be the flaw in this lovely book that allows its soul to breathe.

The one the copyeditor let get away.

Years ago, Taylor came up with a streamer fly that he called the "fall killer." He told me it would catch fish. So I bought a bunch of fall killers from him and went down to the Rio Grande and, by golly, I snagged a batch of hefty lunkers. If Taylor said a fly would catch fish, that fly would catch fish. Guaranteed.

What message do I draw from that observation?

Pure and simple: these stories catch fish.

And all of them are hefty lunkers.

Taos, June 17, 2006

Acknowledgments

■ ■ ■

"Fishing with Nichols" and "Red River Blues" were originally published in *Fly Rod & Reel* magazine. "Rivers of the North" appeared in *High Country* (out of Angel Fire, New Mexico).

Many of the other pieces were in *Horse Fly*—a heroic monthly newspaper in Taos, New Mexico—thanks to Bill Whaley, Nora Anthony, Suzanne de Silva, and Kelly Pasholk.

"Super Fly Sighting" was written by Warren Dean McClenagan.

Garrett VeneKlasen, Mary Lou Polaski, and Gabe Fontanazza contributed photographs.

And for their support and editorial help I would like to thank Tracy McCallum, Kris Edwards, Deb Theodore, John Nichols, Luther Wilson, Garrett VeneKlasen, and the late Gene Berry.

Fall

PART I

NEW MEXICO

CHAPTER ONE

RIVERS OF THE NORTH

■ ■ ■

As a fly-fishing guide I've spent a good deal of my life standing in water: ocean flats, jungle swamps, and Argentine trout rivers. But it's the home rivers of northern New Mexico and southern Colorado that I feel the most connected with. Rivers that, for one reason or another, I have formed close personal relationships with.

Being one of those souls born a couple of hundred years too late, I search for wild spaces to keep my blood flowing. Thankfully, there are still enough waters and woods to explore in the surrounding mountain ranges. When I have looked into every nook and cranny it will be time to move on. But there seems to be little chance of that, because I grow older each year, while the list of waters that I have yet to visit only lengthens.

A lot of the attraction to the area rivers is purely physical, for they pass through a variety of stunning country. The water itself adopts different moods as it drops from the high snowfields. Little ritos giggle as they bounce down from timberline. Then streams turn reflective as they quietly wind through meadows and beaver ponds, to eventually reach their greatest physical strength—after joining forces with other tributaries—when they cut through the sheer rock of canyon walls.

A big part of my connection to the rivers is the wealth of memories gleaned from decades of fishing them. Some of these memories are dramatic, but most are

Rio Grande cutthroat

Brook trout

Sight fishing—man vs. big trout!   *Summer in New Mexico*

just subtle remembrances of nature doing her everyday chores: trout rising for mayflies, violet-green swallows skimming the river, all while mist and cloud form and vanish.

Then there are the remembrances of bizarre events. Whenever I walk by a certain remote section of the Chama River, for instance, I think of the time when a friend and I snuck up on an elk that was grazing beside the river. We got so close that the poor thing fainted in her tracks! Once she regained her senses a little, we sat down beside her and offered our humblest apologies for frightening her so. But our company didn't seem to be helping, and we soon left her to recover on her own.

Dangerous times are hard to forget, too. I remember standing in a creek with a client when the playful tune the stream was singing changed. I wasn't aware of this consciously, but, grabbing his arm, I asked, "Is something different all of a sudden?" We looked at each other, and then upstream, as a flash flood rounded the bend, pushing a roaring wall of water at us. We quickly got out of the stream—but on the wrong

Winter

side—and it wasn't until the water dropped an hour later that we were able to cross back and reach our car.

Moving water can be scary, but it has an inexplicable healing quality, too. I can't really explain what it does to me; but every now and then, when I'm staring mindlessly at the seductive flow, I'm startled to realize—as if for the first time—that this natural wonder of water just never stops. It's forever headed downhill to the mighty sea, and then finds its way back up the mountain to repeat the process all over again. Amazing!

CHAPTER TWO

OLE WALTER

■ ■ ■

Ole Walter was a one-eyed male brown trout that lived a long and solitary life high in the Southern Rockies. I've heard that it is possible for a brown trout to live for more than twenty years. Certainly it took considerable time for him to grow to such great size in a beaver pond at 10,000 feet elevation. But the pond was spring fed and the steady water temperature no doubt lengthened the growing season.

For high drama the pursuit of this spectacular fish falls just short of Captain Ahab's obsessive chase after Moby Dick. But unlike the great white whale—whose defense against his tormentors was the expanse of the seven seas—Walter had to elude capture within the narrow limits of a two-acre beaver pond. And after decades of pacing his watery home, he had developed certain dining habits that made him very difficult to catch.

The pond was well hidden and far from any roads—the kind of place that never gets fished. I first stumbled onto it while on a backpacking trip with friends. I had noticed a rito that had some fresh beaver cuttings in it. I followed the tiny stream up through a dark forest. There were only a few little trout; but there was more beaver sign, so I continued upstream. The rito broke out into an open meadow that snaked by gray skeletons of trees that lay decomposing in the boggy meadow. Sheer peaks surrounded the hidden valley. The quiet of the place was oddly intensified by the muffled roar of a waterfall a mile away. The noise waved off and on with the shifting breezes.

Just beyond the meadow there was a tiny canyon with a beaver dam built right against its rock walls. I remember thinking that it was like the places that men build dams. A great beaver lodge was humped in the center of the pond—and Mr. Beaver himself was lounging up on a hillside close to where the source of this drainage, a

Let me go! Photo by Garrett VeneKlasen

spring, popped out of the ground. The large fellow looked like a slow, lazy monkey, sitting on his butt out in the sun. He waddled into the pond when I took to the bare hill that rose steeply above the little lake. The hill afforded an outstanding view down through the clear water. But after considerable sitting I saw no fish. The beaver must have dammed the spring so close to its source that it was above all the resident fishes. Having nothing better to do, I returned an hour later with a fly rod and relocated a couple of brown trout from the creek below into the pond.

It wasn't until two decades later that I returned to the area with my son, Nick, and a friend of ours, Dr. Leo Ortiz. We were camped a ways away from the pond, and it wasn't until the following morning that I went to see how the fish that I had put in there twenty years before was doing. I expected my planted fish to be long gone, as the beaver cuts on the dam were old and gray now. Mr. B was obviously long gone, but his work lay intact and the pond still looked perfectly fishy. I took the handy hilltop position above the pond. I didn't really expect to see any fish, and I started gazing at the flowers and mountains instead. As I got up to leave, I gave a glance back into the pond just as a huge trout slipped out from under a boulder. It was so long that its body waved snakelike through the water. Wow! I ran back to camp to tell the boys. Manpower would need to be assembled to apprehend the beast.

It didn't take a whole lot of deliberation to get the fellows on the move, and shortly thereafter we approached the hill. With the sun at our backs the leviathan could be plainly seen. And with the help of binoculars we learned that the specimen was a male brown trout. The water was as clear as air, and we could see his spots as he swam by. A scar grazed his side and his belly was burnt orange. We thought we would get him up onshore for a better look and drew straws for who would throw that first, valuable cast.

Nick won, but we all pitched in with ideas about what to use and how to use it. When all was ready, knots tested, cameras prepared, and good luck wishes offered, Nick crept down to the pond. He took out some line, threw a cast out to get his distances in order, and waited. It wasn't long before the big trout's appointed rounds brought him within range. But Nick couldn't see him from water level because of surface glare. Leo and I would have to tell Nick where to cast.

So as not to spook the fish, we would have him place the fly well in front of it. But the first cast was too far in front, and the great trout angled away from the fly. We redirected Nick's cast "fifteen feet left, no, a little more right—add three feet." We were busy watching the fish, but something in Nick's voice made me look at him. He had spotted this trout of a lifetime and the boy's voice and knees were shaking. It looked as if he might wiggle apart and melt to the ground at any minute!

But as the lengthy fellow grew closer, Nick's predatory instincts took over and he naturally made his false casts to the side of the fish so as not to spook it. And when it looked just right Leo and I simultaneously said, "Drop it." It was a perfect cast, five feet in front of the unalarmed animal. The old codger took the slight change of course needed to meet the fly, and then rose upward and, ever so leisurely, passed it by. A communal sigh of "AHHHhaaaa . . ." spread across the calm water of the pond.

Very seldom does a trout that has refused a fly take it on subsequent casts, so we started changing flies. But Ole Walter (by that time he had acquired his legal name) simply wouldn't take anything we offered him. He would give some patterns a better look than others, and we would change accordingly. In other words, if he studied a size sixteen elk hair caddis, we'd think that we were on the right track and show him an eighteen. After he refused such subtle offerings, we'd drag a big whooly bugger by his nose in the hopes of pushing some aggressive button. But unlike us, he never lost his cool.

We scoured one fly box and then another. The maddening thing was that he was obviously feeding—every few feet he would eat something subsurface. Never expecting selective trout in this wild country, we were low on midges (obviously the staple of his diet at this high altitude). But how could you land a fish approaching thirty inches on a midge hook anyway? You couldn't apply enough pressure to steer him away from the rock he lived under, or from the old beaver lodge—both of which sat awkwardly right smack in the middle of the proposed battleground.

When not feeding, he tucked himself under those boulders. It was in the deepest part of the pond. He wasn't a nervous sort and it took a considerable bombardment of casts to run him in there. Over the several years of our relationship, we spent many an hour waiting for him to come out and play. (Nick once backpacked in alone in foul weather and in ten hours of hilltop vigilance only got a ten-minute shot at Wally.)

Each winter we planned our assault. We had pictures of him taken from the hill, and when I looked at them I knew how the vengeful Ahab felt when he reached for his missing leg. Each glance at Walter swimming happily in his watery hole made us tie new flies and greedily sharpen our hooks—with the same determined precision with which the captain sharpened his harpoon. We always wondered if the old boy would make it through another long winter. How thick was the ice? Was our hero getting enough to eat? Would the pond, long abandoned by the beavers, sustain sufficient water to support the aging phenomenon?

One spring day found us on the long trail to Wally's domain. The day was fair, with puffs of white clouds now and then, but no wind ruffled the grasses and flowers. A cow elk moved through the aspens and bleated to her calf. The view of the surrounding peaks was as stunning as it had been twenty years before.

The pond looked about the same, and we took up our usual hilltop position and, with great anticipation, looked for our main man. I remember feeling a little foolish about it all, it being such a singular situation in trout fishing—hiking miles into the wilderness in pursuit of one fish. Who ever heard of such a thing? But when we got our first glimpse of him, we would remember why we came. And sure enough, there he was—the troublemaker himself!—making the rounds of his domain. Nothing had changed except Ole Walter may have added an inch or two to his already long frame. But it was the same story as in previous seasons. We could not get the thing to eat our flies! Man, was it frustrating! Nick did most of the fishing for Walter. He seemed as likely to catch him as I was. His casts fell perfectly in front of the huge brown trout . . . over and over again.

We were pretty well equipped with midges this time and gave him floaters, subsurface models, and an array of tiny larvae. We finally did what we should have done long before—really study the water and Wally's feeding habits. For he always ate the same way—he inhaled things at mid-depth, casually. We got out in the water a ways and discovered that

Don't adjust your eyes—Ole Walter, the elusive one, is too mysterious to focus on.

a particular dark olive midge larva was suspended, head upright, in the water We had him now—or so we thought. We hung various midges from dry flies and the Walster slithered by each morsel in his patented cavalier fashion.

After two days of this we were agitated and turned on each other. My cooking sucked; Nick had better do those GD dishes! We muttered, "Won't it be nice to get home."

I had a miserable night's sleep that night. The altitude and the frustration with Walter were no doubt problems, but vicious dreams of death filled my night. I fell off cliffs, had car accidents, and, scariest of all, was eaten by a shark (no doubt my proper karmic end).

I was surrounded by the subject just then, as my two closest friends had recently been stricken with cancer—within a week of each other. What was so difficult was the way that I learned about the second friend. I'd been gone for a few days, and I called the first guy to ask about the condition of the other. Gene filled me in and then said, "I guess you haven't heard the news about me?" "No," I said. "What news?" He explained that he had had a brain tumor removed three days before and had even less time than our mutual friend Jim. He apologized for breaking this to me, and I, stunned beyond thought and feeling, no doubt said something inadequate and then hung up and plummeted into a deep hole. This backpacking trip was my way of escaping that pain. And catching Ole Walter certainly couldn't hurt.

So, like the obsessive Captain Ahab, I dragged my wasted body toward the great fish, hoping his capture would do more for me than, of course, it could. Leo and Nick were still asleep when I left, not so terribly interested in getting up early to face another day pitted against this slippery genius.

The worst obstacle to landing Wally was the beaver lodge that sat in the middle of the pond. I decided that being on top of it would be the best place to fight him from, because he would be getting pulled on from where I didn't want him to go, and he'd try and go the other way, right? (So much of fishing sounds so good in theory.)

So I waded out there real quiet and looked in the fly box awaiting inspiration. And there it was, the one fly we had somehow overlooked. The fabulous, the one and only—bead head hare's ear nymph number sixteen! And then the beast appeared, not really obvious under a slight chop, and I quickly laid the fly out some ten feet in front of the rascal. He sped up when he spied the fly. Then I lost sight of him and I started retrieving slowly with a hand twist so that I would feel the take. Nothing happened. But I kept it coming, and when he was fifteen or twenty feet away, the bright bead head on the nymph came into sight. When the fly reached the "window" of unruffled water on the leeward side of the beaver lodge, the great beast was following it! My knees began to shake as his huge jaws slowly opened. It was as if I was staring down the gullet of the great whale himself, and the vast whiteness rattled me even further. It took a while for all that to happen; I set the hook before he had closed his mouth on the fly, and I felt the steel scrape across his bony jaw. He turned as if nothing had happened and continued on his way unaffected.

On our final day we couldn't face the humiliation and tried another pond, where we caught a couple of eighteen-inchers. This gave us enough strength to charge back to the pond for one final assault.

Walter was out and about and as cocky as ever. As my son's self-esteem was beginning to suffer from the emotional abuse that this . . . this . . . FISH was handing him, I decided to take the rod. But it was the same old story.

Then, as the light got lower, our boy turned frisky, and instead of cruising his normal midpond grounds, he started prowling the shoreline, swimming fast with a mean look in his eye. As he approached I melted behind a bush and dropped a damsel fly nymph in front of him. It was a totally inappropriate fly for this altitude and time of day; but when I started wiggling it, he charged and ate. And I missed the strike! I immediately slapped it down in front of him, and—when he was but a rod's length away—he grabbed it again.

Incredibly, we were finally fast to the fish. He instantly ran toward the beaver lodge. The 5X tippet wouldn't last long if he got it wrapped around a stick, so I started wading—running was more like it—out toward the beaver lodge. But before I had gone a few steps he changed course and headed straight toward me. I reeled as fast as possible, but I couldn't keep up with him and ran backward up the hill to maintain tension. The great old fish hadn't got all his wits about him as yet, and I figured that maybe we could land him before he knew he was hooked. So I yelled to Nick, "Get him." I kept the pressure on, and Nick scooped him up in his long arms when he reached shore. It looked like Nick was wrestling a gator as the huge fish thrashed about. And I, torn between joy and guilt, yelled excitedly, "Nick, I'm sorry, I wanted you to catch him."

We had forever speculated as to the length of Wally. But we had watched him so long that our estimates of his size would change with our mood. Being landed so green, he was too wild to measure for a while. When he had calmed down, we got the figure—twenty-six and three-quarter inches (to this day the largest trout I have ever caught in the United States). Then we took some photos and released him.

The pictures later showed us something that we had never realized before: the great trout was blind in his right eye. This helped explain why he had refused 10,000 of the 20,000 flies we had offered him!

We knew he survived us, because we watched him prowl the next morning. We returned the following spring and retook our hilltop position to catch the (now thirty-inch?) fish. But we saw neither hide nor hair of our old adversary. Like my friends Gene and Jim, he'd used up his allotted time. We did, however, make some improvements to the aging pond by adding some sticks to the dam. And from the tiny stream below we transplanted a little cutthroat trout into the pond. We considered this an improvement, too. Cutthroats, you see, aren't nearly as difficult to catch as brown trout.

CHAPTER THREE

EGOCENTRICITY

I can't take any more of these festivals! Last week it was the Taos wool festival—THE GREATEST WOOL FESTIVAL EVER! The Outdoor Movie Festival was the week before, and the Mountain Festival is this week—not to mention the endless and ever-so-thrilling art festivals. I'm sure they're all the bestest festivals in the world, but I've lived in Taos too long to feel all that festive—it being my misfortune to know what lies beneath the glitter. Plus, these festives are all younger, richer, and hipper than me—making me feel downright lonely.

And if a guy is gonna feel lonely, he ought to be alone. So I have to find an excuse to get over to Chama. My camper needs to be closed up for the winter. . . . and there are a couple of streams that need observation. But it's so hard to leave this seductive town; something or someone is always about to happen. It just never does. Maybe the woman of my dreams—the bestest gal in the whole world—is fixin' to plunge into my wee world! I can see her now . . . fleeing some distant tragedy and heading straight for salvation under Taos Mountain. And I can almost hear the tires screech as her pink Caddy brakes to a halt at the town limits.

Let's face it, daddy-o, the pink Caddy never seems to stop at my door (although it has crashed through a couple of times). But I have other reasons to stay home: there is an outdoor movie I want to see tonight at the film festival. Hey, wait a minute, I'm choosing to see a movie about the woods rather than actually being there! My thinking seems skewed—must be time to get out of Dodge.

In a couple of hours I have made the necessary phone calls, taken my mom to the market, and pointed the jeep west. I always feel better once I get across the gorge bridge. Although the vibes of the Taos Hum have now extended past there, the quiet

Serenity interrupted—Chama, New Mexico

of the sagebrush still dominates. (If anyone reading this is unfamiliar with the Taos Hum—unlikely, because it is the bestest hum in the whole world—let me explain. A certain part of the valley was said to be humming some years back. Many of us who were familiar with the area deduced that an electrical substation there was responsible, but experts were summoned from around the globe and that simplistic theory was debunked.)

Once beyond the hum zone I regain ownership of my mind, and I'm free to plan my weekend as I choose. I have to get to my first destination quickly, because it's a creek with big spawners, but I won't be able to see them unless there is sunlight and the day is getting on—so I put the cruise control on giddy up, take off my shoes, and proceed into the mountains.

When I reach the creek I get the waders on quickly, as I still have a good walk to reach the best pools. I go over a little hill and surprise a young antelope. Unusual to see one at 10,000 feet this late in the year (October). The little animal lopes up the opposing slope and turns blazing white when it steps into the late sunlight. This is summer range, and the kid has obviously lost its way back to the lowlands. It stops every few feet to look back at me, and I try to imagine how it will negotiate its way through all that forest and back to the plains in its glaring uniform. A coyote will probably hamstring it. As it trots under a big rock outcropping I wonder if a red fox could bring it down; I saw a litter of them here this summer. My client and I had quit fishing to watch them play outside their den. They carried on as if they were starring in a Taos outdoor movie festival. The mom stood sentry from atop a rock outcropping while the pups wrestled and chased each other right below her.

The foxes seem to be gone, and after bidding the antelope adieu I turn and keep heading up the stream. But it has grown late, and my shadow is so long now that it crosses some fish; they flush from their spawning beds. With the light so low I can't see in the water, I start studying the flat shallow stream ahead for movement. I do see a push of water; and since I have had no luck with the hopper I have been fishing, I put on a black unweighted whooly bugger—hard to beat for spawning browns and the bestest last-resort fly I know of. When I get to where I saw the push I get down low and make a cast short of where I think the fish is. It comes across the shallow pool making a V wake like a submarine on attack. The eighteen-inch brown intercepts the intruder, and I set the hook when I see the line tighten. It doesn't take long to land because it is thin and spawned out.

I move upstream and jump some Mexican ducks. I think that's what they are—both genders of Mexican ducks look like the much more common hen mallard. It would be against the law of averages to see a group of hen mallards with no greenhead drakes, so I deduce that they are Mexican ducks, a relatively rare species that is seen only at the beginning of fall migration. (Although I enjoy seeing, hearing, and eating them, I'm not a real birder—which my less-than-scientific identification process attests to.)

I come up to a big boulder with a small but deep hole on the upstream side of it. The spot looks too cramped for a good fish to turn around in; but hiding places are few and far between in this sparse stream, and when I send my whooly bugger in to investigate, a good fish instantly nails it. It is about the same size as the other trout but in great shape, a male in its full spawning dress, with a yellow belly and big red spots that leap out, sporting a hook jaw that makes it look mean as a snake.

It's the end of a long day, at the end of a long fishing season, and I'm bored with fishing and head back. I'm watching above me for elk as I go, and way upslope I see a group emerge into the sunlight and then walk through some brilliant golden aspens. One is bigger and lighter colored than the others and I suspect it is a bull, but I can't see the horns from this distance. When it starts hassling the other elk it gives away its gender. They disappear for a while in some trees, and a lone cow appears again much closer. I make a lame cow call—without the aid of a real store-bought call—and the cow stares at me and steps back into the forest.

That concludes the daylight activity, and I arrive in Chama about dark. I'm surprised to see the sidewalks and streetlights finished. Nice enough, but I hope it isn't so cute that it draws more people. Chama is too funky a town for most city folks, and I would hate to see that change. If Taos is the sizzle, Chama is the beef. It's a naturalist's dream; if when driving through the middle of town you see an animal crossing the road, it is as likely to be wild as it is to be domesticated. Geese and osprey fly overhead, moose and lynx have moved in, and the last grizzly in the southern Rockies was killed not thirty miles from here some twenty years ago. The elk and deer population is incredible, and during fall I have heard elk bugle from Main Street.

But beef has its gristle, and when I arrive at my camper I toss out dead mice that ate the poison I left out for them. I push the window back in place that a bear broke through last year. Bears are a real problem, and that window cost a couple of hundred bucks. Earlier this summer I was awakened at 3 a.m. to the sight of a black something sliding up the window not four feet away. Now, at that dreamy hour I'm usually not sure what is real and what's not, but when a big black snout followed into view, I knew that it was not a dream and that the first object I'd seen was the bear's paw. I started yelling and pounding on the wall and that ran the bear off. There is this ever-present need to deal with the throes of reality in Chama—but I find it less traumatic than deciding which world-class event to attend in Taos.

The next day I'm meeting a friend and we are going to fish a secret spot on the Chama River. We park the car and hike a mile, and then head down into the river's canyon. I have heard that there are some big fish present, and the black whooly bugger I still have on should work. I'm high up on a rock and on my first cast a two-pound rainbow starts after the fly. I slow up the retrieve to let him catch it, and when his mouth closes on the fly I set the hook. Strong from the cool fall water, the fish jumps several times. I'm thinking that this is gonna be great, and then I don't get a strike in the next few pools. It's the catching-a-fish-on-the-first-cast-is-bad-luck syndrome. My companion is just sitting back and watching—the way women so easily do.

We have lunch under the pines. When we emerge the weather has improved to cloudy, and this has brought the mayflies out—and several trout are rising in the next pool.

I reach for a fly box and, as is my habit, I also check on the valuables pocket while I'm there. My wallet isn't home, and I hunt through the vest and backpack and then look around the lunch spot, but it isn't there either. And then I kind of remember laying it on the back bumper. The car is parked beside a quiet stretch of highway where with luck no one will happen on it . . . and fish are rising everywhere. What to do—what to do? Julie hasn't even fished yet, so I make a compromise and decide to fish just this pool in front of us. We can clearly see a twelve-inch rainbow; and when she gets a cast over it, the fish heads upward, opens its mouth, and eats something just an inch from her fly. I make a few casts at fish that are rising too far off for her to reach. But I'm distracted about the wallet and do poor work, spooking several nice fish. We scram back to the car, where the wallet awaits us on the back bumper. It is almost worth losing stuff to experience the relief that comes when you find that it was never lost.

I head home the next morning by way of a fishing and elk-hunting spot that I want to inspect for my son's upcoming bull hunt. We have a number of remote fishin' holes that we seldom guide, but I make the rounds anyway to see if the road has changed and make sure that the stream isn't strewn with empty bait containers. I have tried to phrase it so that it sounds like it is really my job; the truth is that visiting these wild places is what makes the job—and life—palatable.

It is hard to describe what makes someplace wild for me. A wild spot could loosely be defined as one where no one goes unless they have business there: hunting, fishing, or looking for lost stock. But some country gets visited more frequently and still main-tains its integrity. So it's hard to define "wild"; there are just some places here on earth where I feel extra alive, free, and peaceful all at the same time.

This is an out-of-the-way spot and the road fades to faint and then to dead as it ends at the rim of a valley. There is a meadow below, and a tiny lake sits right in the middle of it. Apparently nobody has figured out how to get logs out of the valley, because huge ponderosas surround the field. I walk down the elk trail to an overlook. There are no human tracks, but there are elk tracks of various ages. The bull elks love this place, and once, when I was here with clients, we found the ground scraped as if a sharp stick had been working on it. Then we noticed hoof marks and realized that bulls had been fighting and their horn tips had carved up the ground. Later in the afternoon we saw a bull wallowing and pissing in a mud hole on the side of the little lake. Seems that girl elk can't resist a studly bull glazed over with mud and urine.

But it would be a lot of work hauling meat up and out of there, and I have heard from a hunting confidant that there are elk on a big rocky mountain nearby. (A hunting/fishing confidant is someone who can keep his mouth shut and knows the same number of secret places as you do.) I drive up toward this mountain of rock and then set off on foot.

There is elk sign but a lot of wild horse sign, too. In places the horses have eaten almost every blade of grass in sight. They are pretty shy, but the few I've seen can only be described as blue in color. Not like the wild horses out on the prairie—prehistoric-looking brown beasts—these are noble creatures and look like they just stepped off of the winner's circle at Belmont. But they are still feral animals ruining the range of the native deer and elk. They live in the thick forest here, I assume, because ranchers probably shoot at them when they get out in the open. You'd get twenty years in the pen for killing one because of the Wild Horse Act. The people who made the wild horse laws are no doubt enamored with the idea of mustang manes flying in the breeze—while I swear at tripping over a huge pile of horseshit.

Even though it is raining, snowing, and icing all at the same time, I'm interested in seeing this country, and I start hiking all around this huge rock of a mountain. But the night's gloom is advancing prematurely, and I decide that I'd better head back to the car.

I reach the track that I believe my car is parked near and start down it. After I have walked a ways without seeing my tracks or anything familiar, I start to feel panic welling up in my chest. I tell myself that I can't really get lost because this is the only road here. "Or so you think," says the fear. But I'm deeply snakebit after my hairy experience a couple of years before on the Sierra Alto (see chapter 20), and being back in a similar situation finds me getting uncontrollably scared.

The fear shouts, "Turn around and head back in the opposite direction"; but fortunately something makes me whirl back onto my original course. But fear tries again and adds, "The precipitation may have washed out the car tracks and I will never find the car." (I did foolishly park it well off the road among some trees.) I pick up a twig and try to snap it to see if fuel would be dry enough to build a fire; but it is so wet that it just bends. By now the panic has affected my breathing, so I force myself to breathe deeply. But I get more out of focus with each step—almost dizzy. I try the cell phone, but there is no signal; and then I see that the area ahead looks familiar. I cross my almost-washed-out tire tracks and exhale a vast sigh of relief. Finding that I'm not lost is even more thrilling than finding that my wallet wasn't lost the day before.

All in all, it's been a good weekend, so I head back to Taos to see what's been invented since I left. But my time in the wilderness has left me unprepared for the hum zone, and I make the mistake of turning on the local radio; two real estate ads culminate in a crescendo of greed with the gruff voice of Harry Blastem. My peaceful world of birds and bees further crumbles as I see a troop of drainbow people decked out in full drab. Then some bikers whiz by, all conforming to black nonconformity. Then the radio station informs me that it is "world famous"—lest I had forgotten over the weekend. (It must be the bestest, because I've never heard another station say this.) Then a sign declares that Taos is the "Soul of the Southwest."

I've returned an innocent, and all the hubbub is working its magic on me. And as I hum along beneath sacred Taos Mountain, my head buzzes with world-class ideas. Just an hour ago I was off in the forest empty-headed and of little use to myself or my fellow man. But now, as I'm reminded that I'm in "the solar capital of the world," inspiration overtakes. We here in Taos have harnessed about every kind of energy there is, but the one thing that Taos is way long on is psychic energy. If that stuff is gonna be harnessed, it will be here. And then I move past brilliant—to pure genius! The Taos Hum is simply the collective ego of the entire town? So happy with itself that it hums! And if we could harness it, we could put it in some kind of usable form. We could call it . . . ah hah! EGOCENTRICITY! Yes, that's it—egocentricity, the bestest form of energy in the whole dang world!

A "hum catcher" could be put over certain hot spots; suspend the device under the high ceiling at the Taos Inn on a Saturday night, for instance. If the amount of egocentricity falls, extra concho belts and sharp black hats could be handed out, thereby raising the level of profiling.

There could be personal and social benefits as well. For if I was responsible for relieving the massive ego of Taos, I might get to live in a normal, unpretentious town—making me the bestest person here!

Chapter Four

RED RIVER BLUES

▨ ▨ ▨

Introduction

The Red River tumbles into the Rio Grande fifteen miles above Taos, New Mexico. The last few miles of the river cut through a parched, deep, and nasty canyon composed of vertical cliffs, jumbled rock, dense brush, and cholla cactus. Below this tangle of trouble an equally unruly ribbon of white water smashes its way to the awaiting Rio Grande. Its official federal classification as a wild river seems appropriate—if the matter of mining pollution is disregarded.

The lower Red has the natural ingredients of a perfect trout stream. From the Red River State Hatchery (located at the mouth of the canyon) downriver, numerous springs dump, trickle, and pour into the river. These springs stabilize the flow and the water temperature, thereby allowing the fish (and aquatic insects) to prosper year round. And as the Red dashes to meet the Rio Grande, the churning of the water adds essential oxygen. There are deep, shaded holes for big trout and gravel beds for spawning. And on top of that, nature gets a boost from man (rare indeed!) as the fish hatchery adds nutrients to the river. It would be hard to dream up a more ideal stream.

My first trip into the lower Red was in 1969. I bushwhacked my way from the hatchery downriver into what I thought would be total wilderness. I didn't expect that the designation "wild river" meant that there would be metal buildings at the end of groomed switchback trails. I, an innocent—and ignorant—refugee from the east, also assumed that this "wild river" term meant that you could drink the water. Which I did, and becoming very ill, turned thankful that I had a nice metal hut to lay up in. I was starting to see how this "wild river" business worked. (And mind you that this was considerably BEFORE the river became "polluted.") I spent two miserable days there,

The clear water of the lower Red River, circa 1980. Photo by Mary Lou Polaski

finally crawling out on a deer trail and hitchhiking back to my home, New Buffalo Commune. Not much of a fishing trip.

The water I consumed looked OK; in fact, the river usually ran clear back then. At that time the pollution generally came from the concentrated punch of "slurry breaks." This was not an uncommon event, as the pipelines that passed along the river would rupture from the friction of conveying the highly abrasive ore. So before dropping into the canyon I would always check on the color of the water from a lookout on the rim. But more than once I arrived at the river at about the same time as a spill. It is one thing to get skunked by natural causes—bad weather, high water, depressed fish—but when the willful hand of man is the culprit . . . it would make for some pretty long walks back up the steep trail—dragging my heavy heart behind me.

Down on the Red

I have a fond recollection of fishing the lower Red River canyon on an early spring day some thirty years ago. Probably April, that wonderful time of year when the mountains are still white but the scents of spring are adrift on the warm air below. A great time to fish, a time when—after the long fasts of winter for fish and fisherman—the big trout are ravenous and as frantic to be caught as the impatient fisher is to catch them. A time before mining had polluted the lonely river . . .

With backpack loaded with food and fishing gear, I descended toward the white ribbon of water below. I was headed for a camping spot beyond any visible trail. A bench I had seen from the rim looked special, if for no other reason than that it was the only level place in that steep world. After negotiating a rugged mile of cliff and cactus, I finally reached the spot and swung my pack to the ground.

What a beautiful, wild place, as two-foot-thick ponderosas spread shade, vanilla scent, and soft needles over the oasis. A twenty-foot-high boulder stood on end among the great trees. The rock had a natural chimney—an indentation that carried smoke up and away. Even the roar of the crashing river below had been tamed by passing through this little paradise, giving it just the right gurgle to ensure proper sleep. I ended up using the place often and eventually stashed some cooking gear there to lighten the load when hiking in and out.

The fishing was wild, and every pool gave up a trout from one to three pounds. It was a workout, because each powerful fish sought escape by running downriver, and I'd have to give chase, getting not only soaked but bashed and bruised on the rocks as well. I got tired of the treatment and decided to put on a stout tippet, stand my ground, and haul the bastards upstream. Sure enough, the next trout I hooked sped for the Rio Grande. I tried to get him airborne—figuring that once he was out of his element I could skip him upriver—I heaved, and the glass fly rod broke below the ferrule.

What a spot that put me in. Big trout on a suicidal rampage and I was sitting in camp, unarmed. I couldn't take it, and before long was out in the river flailing away with my snub-nosed fly rod. Right off, just in front of camp, I hooked an absolutely huge cutbow of no less than five pounds. It tore downriver, stopped, and then jumped high above the water. The jump created slack line that looped around the splintered end of the stick. So when it rushed off again, and the line pulled tight, it snapped. The monster was gone. I took a few deep, trembling breaths and decided to hack off the last few inches of the rod. I broke it off down to the second eye so I wouldn't get wrapped again and continued fishing. Not with the graceful ten to two strokes of the noble fly caster, but with a wild slashing motion that sent the flies winging in a wide arc. And many of these ugly casts were necessary when fishing for those big fish, because the fly needed to be placed in various spots at the heads of the deep pools in the hopes that one of those drifts would run the fly in front of the deep holding fish. It was tough to cover the water effectively because I couldn't muster the necessary accuracy to get the fly where I wanted it. And since the end of my rod was now several more feet away from the action, I couldn't stick the rod out over the fly to get a good drift. But somehow, in spite of it all, they were so hungry that I ended up landing three nineteen-inchers.

On another trip I fished a certain deep pool in a remote area of the Red that held a large cutbow. The hole was just upstream of a huge log that had fallen across the river. It was a big Doug fir suspended just a few inches above the rushing water. Underneath, the log had been clean-shaven by the river, but dense, long branches protruded from the top and sides.

The first time I fished the pool I hooked a hog that ran off downriver—as is their fashion. I followed until the log stopped me. From that point I watched helplessly as line peeled off the reel. Then I tried a maneuver that I had read about someplace; I think that the tactic was designed for fighting huge runaway salmon. I yanked line off

Note the blue tint of the modern-day Red River.

the reel as fast as possible, giving the fish slack—the idea being that the current would carry the fly line below the ignorant creature, looping below the fish. Theoretically, when the line pulled from the other direction, the fish would lose track of the crafty angler and stop.

It seemed to work—the line went slack anyway—and either I had lost him or he was stopped. But I was on the wrong side of the log; and if our boy was still hooked, he was way downstream. Literally—around a bend I could see through the branches. Anything for such a fish! So I gulped some air, held my nose with one hand and the rod with the other, and under the log I dove. I bobbed back up to the surface and splashed on downstream, reeling up slack as I went. I wanted to get down below the fish so we would be far from that log when we started fighting again, in case he should decide to head home. I passed below where the line was hanging in the current to something—the fish, I supposed. Then I reeled up tight and renewed the struggle. Before long the great fish and I lay gasping for air on a gravel beach. After killing and stashing the beast I spread tobacco, wallet, and other drenched articles in the sun to dry.

From then on, whenever I fished that pool, I stripped for the possible swim—removing vest, shirt, hat, sunglasses, cigarettes, and matches, and placing them next to the log before making my first cast.

I wasn't too good an influence back then on the Red. It was long before the days of catch-and-release, and I sacked hordes of huge trout. But in the end, my crimes paled to insignificance compared with the effects of the upstream mining of molybdenum.

Although the Moly Mine had a negative influence on the Red for a long time, the rich river had held its own until the intense ore extractions of the eighties. Then, in the blink of an evolutionary eye, fish populations went to almost nothing in the smelly soup. The destruction was so devastating that even years later the river is still but a tainted blue-green version of its former self.

And although it seems to become healthier each year, the fishery falls far short of its potential. The mighty resident cutbows are gone and the river is now inhabited by smallish brown trout and pellet-brained rainbows donated from the hatchery above.

I guided a fellow down that remote area of the Red recently. I hadn't been there in a long time, and there is a pretty good trail now by the place I used to camp. After he had caught about twenty small browns, he looked at me with a grin and said, "Pretty good, isn't it?"

But I, lost in a lonely vision of great red trout leaping out of the clear water, could only respond with a faint "uh-huh."

CHAPTER FIVE

MY VALLE VIDAL

Since I'm a permit holder in the Valle Vidal, I was asked to say a few words about the place.* Hopefully I will represent some of the other fishing guides, since we share similar experiences and needs. Between us we have collectively taken a lot of people fishing there. I am also the author of a book called *Fly Fishing New Mexico*; and since I wrote so warmly of the place, I have probably influenced others to fish there as well.

I was on the expedition that drove through the Valle Vidal just after it became the property of the people of the United States. That was twenty-some years ago and the group included some very enthusiastic Forest Service folks, and potential permittees like myself. We stopped by the line camp on Costilla Creek and I walked up to the cave that overlooks the stunning valley. There were ancient smoke stains above the cave showing that I wasn't the first one to admire the view. There was a badger hole right at the entrance, and on top of the pile of excavated dirt was a perfect obsidian arrowhead.

Back then the fishing was for large Rio Grande cutthroats. They aren't as big now as they were then, but the Valle Vidal is still one of the few easy-access public fisheries that's good enough to guide on. It's everyman's stream, not just because there are lots of fish, but also because its gentle nature makes it perfect for both young and old. I've even had handicapped people catch fish there. It's great for beginners, and it's where thousands of would-be fly fishers have caught their first trout.

---

* This speech was originally given at a Forest Service hearing in January 2005 concerning drilling for coalbed methane on the Valle Vidal unit of the Carson National Forest in northern New Mexico.

Costilla Creek

Part of the uniqueness of the Valle Vidal is that it is one of just a few wild and unspoiled areas that is accessible to the public. When I take Mr. John Q. Public to inspect his property, the first thing I point out is the fine condition of the land. In fact, the change is immediate once you cross the cattle guard and enter the Valle Vidal, because the streamside vegetation is waist-deep with sedges, tall grass, and wildflowers. Willows and alder shade the creek and pines march up the slopes in back—which is, I would imagine, pretty much the way God intended it to be. I often point out to my clients that the Valle Vidal is a special unit of the forest and is managed with kid gloves. Besides being lightly grazed, it is illegal to keep a single fish you catch in the streams, and the area is off-limits until July because of elk calving. And although the elk calving regulation

Valle Vidal, New Mexico—protected forever

seems especially silly when present threats are considered, the Carson Forest people should be commended for their fine stewardship of the land—thus far.

Guiding is allowed by permit, and it is an important source of income for many local fishing (and hunting) guides. But this isn't an economic pitch—if economics were my strong suit, I wouldn't be in the fishing business. My real relationship with the Valle Vidal comes after the workday—when those happy new fly fishermen head back to Taos and I'm left with an hour or two of my own. I seldom fish, although I might like to catch a Rio Grande cut from Comanche Creek, as they are close to being genetically pure, and each one has its own unique spotting and colorations. I might take my camera and lie down in the grass to get a shot of some flowers with the snows of Costilla Peak in the background. I know which places the elk like and will be on the lookout for them as I go. And I'm always on the watch for birds; one time I came upon an elk carcass with five eagles on it. Various birds of prey often spiral south of Comanche Point, and by the Costilla there are western tanagers in the trees and dippers bobbing in the creek.

Occasionally I'll drive over to the Shuree Ponds and take a walk down to the kids' lake where my son, Nick, caught his first big trout twenty years ago. I think about what it must have been like there when Clark Gable and that Hollywood crowd were at the lodge. And I picture all the huge elk that must have been hung from the great meat poles in front of the house. I got my own elk out of the famous Valle Vidal herd. My pal Tracy and I dragged her about a mile downhill, and then had to reduce her to quarters to make it up the tiny slope by the road.

But the older I get, the less I care about hunting, catching fish, counting birds, or keeping any kind of score when I'm outside. I've come to realize that I need silence more than accomplishments. So usually after work, I just drive a mile or two, go for a walk in no particular direction, and expect nothing in particular to happen.

That nothing is still available in the Valle Vidal. Let's hope it remains so. It's a rare commodity these days.

Author's Note: Legislation permanently protecting the Valle Vidal from oil and gas development was passed in Washington in the fall of 2006.

John Nichols hugs a Rio rainbow.

PART II

RIO GRANDE

Chapter Six

FISHING WITH NICHOLS

■ ■ ■

John Nichols is not a lazy man. He hikes, fishes, or hunts almost every day, and then writes all night. Folks here in Taos, New Mexico, know his schedule and don't molest him until after 2 p.m. But there are exceptions—and this is fishin'—so I ring him out of bed at noon. When I get to his house a half hour later, he is set to go, loaded with sandwiches, Cokes, and fishing gear. We take my car as it is newly repaired (my ace mechanic has the engine knock down to where I only have to turn the radio up halfway to "fix" it); John's thirty-year-old Dodge truck is in the shop. I, new to the writing racket and used to the riches of fly-fishing guiding, ask the seasoned writer if he thinks Michael Crichton's car is in the shop. He chuckles while throwing his stuff in the back and smirks, "Michael Crichton can't catch trout."

What's more the pity is that John is a successful writer. He claims to have written eighty books, but only seventeen have been published. Three have been made into movies: *The Milagro Beanfield War*, *The Wizard of Loneliness*, and *The Sterile Cuckoo*. He has written endless magazine pieces, speeches, and essays. John holds forth on a lot of different subjects: ecology, communism, the blues, Latin American politics, his crummy health, women, men, and rural Hispanic life in Northern New Mexico. Raised "all over the place," he is fluent in French and Spanish and speaks English with, as he puts it, "tolerable locution."

John puts a lot of life into all his work, but when he writes of fly-fishing the rough and tumble Rio Grande gorge, the words spring off the page into wondrous images of a wild and beautiful place. Listen to his passion for the Rio Grande in these lines from *The Last Beautiful Days of Autumn*: "I love it. Every last fatal, traumatic, and bewitching moment of my time on the Rio Grande. On each new trip, when I arrive at the rim and gaze down, it is like reaching the other side of a magic mountain and viewing a scene toward which my imagination has strained for ages."

This is a special trip for both of us because it's the first time we have ever fished together. We've been friends for thirty years and talked fishing a hundred times, always threatening to get together and do it. But our worlds seldom collide. He's up all night writing that stack of books while I'm out guiding. So, as we drive north toward Questa, we have a lot to catch up on and are jabbering away. We parallel the river as we go, and each time we get in the proximity to a trail we tell each other stories about the place: tales of big fish, nasty falls, flash floods, and rabid beavers. John is especially well versed on the trails in "the box," a fifteen-mile section of canyon that few people have the audacity to fish. Places like Rope Trail, Rattlesnake, and the Devil's Crotch. (Place names have been changed—or invented—to protect the innocent. Actually, you'd never find any of these bajadas without John—or the handful of other fishermen that know them.)

As we pass the Gorge Bridge, John talks about a long riffle above the bridge where he once pulled out "an endless number" of fish. The trail to it is a narrow slice and slide down an almost sheer cliff that starts below the famous bridge. I ask if, when he walks under the bridge, tourists ever throw stuff down at him. "Do they?" he says. "All the time, and missiles get going pretty good after 600 feet. I've even thought of wearing a hard hat!"

We come to a trail that neither of us has fished much. I take advantage of the lull in our animated conversation and apply the brakes. John says, "Sure, this is fine."

Like any unimproved trail on the Rio Grande, it's steep and dangerous; but it leads to bountiful water. And best of all, it's untouched by the mischievous hand of man. But it's midafternoon, a poor time to angle in this warm weather, so we assemble our packs without rushing. We open a couple of Cokes and fiddle with our stuff. It's hard to get anything done standing next to this striking part of the canyon. It's like being beside a gorgeous woman—the view is so stunning that your head just keeps spinning back toward her. To the north, perfectly round Ute Mountain rises above the canyon.

Looming beyond that is jagged Mount Blanca, covered in snow. The water below has a golden sheen from the sun's reflection off the far canyon wall. Several tall Douglas firs stand silhouetted against a long pool on the river.

After working with John on the film version of *Milagro*, Robert Redford called him a "true rebel." The Orvis clothes designers might say the same of his fly-fishing attire—if they were in a gracious mood. He's got on black and white "jogger special" sneakers and paint-smeared pants; a jacket tied around his waist has a huge gash with white stuffing oozing out. A turquoise cap, faded fishing vest, and aluminum net complete the ensemble. Always one to stomp on ceremony, John wrote in *The Last Beautiful Days of Autumn*, "the genteel image of the aristocratic angler is further savaged."

John and I continue to praise the temperamental river as we leisurely descend the steep trail. All of sudden, though, once he gets a whiff of the water, my friend's pace picks up and his manner changes. Again, from *The Last Beautiful Days Of Autumn*: "Never have I approached the river on any fishing afternoon except with a bounding excitement in my heart, an incredibly powerful lust to reach the water and begin, and an absolute faith that this day could be my best ever."

When we reach the river, John gets a worried look on his face as he searches in his knapsack for his reel. He forgot it, and he explores elsewhere for his spare. He pulls a huge Pfleuger Medalist from some deep pocket in his clownlike apparel. It's "the size of a frying pan," but will do. It has an eight-weight bright orange line on it that is as thick as your finger.

Forgetfulness, catastrophes, and outrageous incidents occur to everybody who fishes this wild canyon on a regular basis. And as John assembles his tuna reel to his rod, "the first graphite ever made," he remembers an event that happened in the pool right in front of us. He was with his now departed pal and fishing nemesis, outdoor writer Mike Kimmel. "Seems as if we were about even in the fish tally that day—we were very competitive when fishing together. Just as we were about to head up the trail, I hooked a very big cutbow over there. Claiming that I had raided 'his' pool, Kimmel started throwing rocks at the fish and, when that didn't succeed, he tackled me. I fended him off with one hand while fighting the fish with the other. Of course I landed the trout anyway—a twenty-incher."

John has a long list of atrocities that the river has dealt him—well documented in his books. He once carried a girlfriend with a broken ankle up out of the canyon—at 3 a.m.! He's lost glasses, fly boxes, knives; a whole rod and reel was once sacrificed to the drink. Many rods have been broken on these hard basalt stones. But John has a motto to cover such losses: "If you buy it cheap, you don't weep." On another occasion his cowboy companion sat on a bed of cactus and John spent hours removing the spines from his pal's butt.

Without doubt, the most perilous part of a trip into the canyon is the trip out. To raise the stakes—and, he hopes, catch lots of fish at this prime time—John usually assaults the rim at the latest possible hour. *In The Last Beautiful Days Of Autumn* he writes:

> On Suicide Slide, for example, there's nothing to do but claw my way straight up. It's dark, visibility is near zero. One hand is occupied with my rod case; my other hand grapples for plants, which often tear loose from the steep bank. Heavy fish in my gunny sack looped around a backpack shoulder-strap bash against my ankle. A bush has so much resin on it that my fingers are quickly glued together. Traversing helps little: rocks constantly rumble from under my feet. Half a dozen times I pitch rocks ahead to warn rattlers of my approach. Tonight several of those rocks bounce back at me, and I have to duck quick to avoid a braining by my own missile. Shaken, I figure it's better to probe ahead with the rod case—tap, tap, tap . . . you there, snakes? Please don't strike. I promise not to hurt you. . . .

As John and I start downriver, we come across a big wooden sign erected by the Bureau of Land Management. It is not obvious, and I had never noticed it before. It declares that there are dangerous rapids below and boaters should go no further. John figures that the sign was probably erected about twenty years ago, after some out-of-state college kids thought they would float this "unrunable" section of the river in a rubber raft. The spring flood flung them to their deaths against the stones, and only one of the six crawled out alive. "Gotta respect the river," John says. And then mutters, "I hate rafters."

John "I Hate Rafters" Nichols points to a sign and says,
"If you are zipping by here in a raft, you'll probably never
notice this. If you do, you had better have good eyesight
and be a fast reader!"

With that he starts skipping from one rock to the next with the same heedless exu-
berance that cost those departed teenagers their lives. Listen to his first paragraph from
the story "Down on the Rio Grande": "Where it is difficult I go the most. Narrow trails
winding down steep inclines carry me to water that roars between countless slippery
boulders. When I leap across those rocks I feel more alive than at any other time."

John very often fishes the river by himself. Now that would sound like a sufficient
challenge for most sixty-year-old men who have undergone open-heart surgery, but
John's deteriorating physical condition goes that one better. He has Méniére's disease,
and that ups his handicap considerably. He gets dizzy and often loses his balance. This
whirling disease may even cause him to black out. In just the last few minutes I've seen
him almost topple over twice. And as I watch him bounce downriver, he spins, totters
for a second—this way and that—and turns the near fall into a net gain of a yard by
using his momentum to stumble ahead. Graceful he ain't.

When we get amid a massive boulder field, John rigs up. He fishes the Rio the old way: with two wet flies. He learned this style—as I did—from longtime Taoseño and Rio Grande king Charley Reynolds. The method employs a brown and a black wet in sizes ten and twelve. (Think of a dirty pipe cleaner wrapped on a hook with a bit of hackle at the head.) The dropper is tied on the tag end of a blood knot, and when fished properly the tail fly swims in the water while the dropper bounces and jiggles across the surface. This sexy act taunts the Rio Grande's unsophisticated trout, and sometimes, even after many passes, they succumb to temptation and glom onto it. Of course the fish need to be up and on the prowl for this to work really well, which pretty much limits the wet fly man to the evening hours. I suggest to John that he might be better off fishing nymphs deep at other times of the day. He says he knows that but can't get up to fish earlier, and he hates nymphing anyway. Plus his idea of success is "scarcity, not plethora. If I made this too easy, it wouldn't be half the fun."

Once rigged up, John starts pounding the water like Rambo on a rampage. He leans over, very intense, raises a small fish in the first hole and yells, " Had one—ten-inch brown." The hand fly bobs and weaves around the front of a boulder and wham!—another trout—a bigger rainbow—smashes at it but misses. Things are looking good. But, about that time, the weather turns turbulent and John takes a dubious glance at a dark cloud that has just prowled over the canyon wall. "A mysterious storm materializes," he writes in *Autumn*, "the barometer nose-dives, and, their jaws wired shut, a million hungry trout, with aggravated indifference, watch my cleverly wiggled offering swoop by."

He fishes along—doing all sorts of maneuvers with his rod, raising it high in one spot to reach over a huge boulder, then mending a hunk of thick orange line over a smaller rock. He completes the cast by jiggling the rod upright again so the flies will hang in a foam eddy. He repeats the complicated procedure a few times and then wisely tries the pool from a different angle. Nada.

The Rio Grande is a fine natural trout river, loaded with big fish. But such rich streams also have lots of food, and the fat boys don't need to feed all the time. In fact, sometimes—some days, some hours—it may feel like the fish will never eat. Another truth about this river is that the larger fish—usually wild cutbows in extremely good condition—are easily lost in battle. When the mass of a three-pounder heads downriver, over waterfalls and around boulders, it is hard to hold. This doesn't bother

John—he only gets more inspired when the going get tough. He sums up his attitude pretty well in "Down on the Rio Grande": "You bastard! I cry, my entire body aquiver with trout loss dismay syndrome—the worst (and most wonderful) pain on earth. And as I sit there gasping, laughing, and cursing my flawed technique, I feel so high on the intensity of the low that anything else is an anticlimax."

John carries this benevolently masochistic attitude into another pursuit as well. When I tell him that I have had a great grouse season and killed a pile of them with little effort, he replies, "A perfect day for me grouse hunting is when I walk for six hours and flush just one. If I get it I'm triumphant, but if I don't—well, that's fine, too." John takes the month of September off, and in tribute to that wonderful time in New Mexico he wrote his novel *An Elegy for September*. A girl in the book figures the main character out pretty well when she says of his grouse shooting, "You'll deliberately miss on purpose."

John and I have more laughs than fish the rest of that stormy afternoon. I get some pinup photos of him climbing a ladder that had washed downriver—intact somehow—from distant Colorado. We eat our sandwiches across the river from a huge spring that gushes out of the canyon wall. It plunges into the Rio in a series of short waterfalls. I haven't brought enough drinking water and tell John that I'm going to try to get across the river to get some. He offers to share his meager supply with me but warns that if he doesn't have enough he'll go into atrial fibrillation and die. I lie and tell John that I don't really need the water. But later, when he fishes around the bend, I make the tricky crossing to get my water. It seems like a better option than carrying the heavyweight author out of the canyon—while dying of thirst myself.

As we fish into the twilight we eagerly pump each other with the lines that our optimistic sport employs: "as soon as the wind stops"—"when we reach that pool"—"if you can't get one there" . . . you know the list. A few rebellious fish attack briefly and John does land one nice cutbow. But all in all, it's a slow day for the Rio.

As we head up the trail, I'm feeling a little subdued about the day's fishing. I'm a pro and expected the fish to respond accordingly for this special occasion. We stop to catch our breath when we are about halfway to the top. A few stars twinkle through clouds that race over the rim. I bitch about the problematic trout. John shakes his head in a way that suggests he isn't offended by the day's results. "The process" he blurts, between deep breaths, "is everything."

CHAPTER SEVEN

COLLEEN

■ ■ ■

The phone rings at 7:30 and the first subject is the day's menu—Colleen's got the bread and cheese and I have the meat, mustard, and some of the neighbor's apples. We are planning to fish the upper Rio Grande, and we discuss whether we have the strength to take two cars and fish from one rugged trail to another. We decide that that is too brutal an idea and opt for something a little less intense—but still a nine on the Rio's degree-of-difficulty scale.

I've been guiding fly fishermen every day for what seems like the whole summer, and I'm a little nervous that my day off will be spent guiding Colleen as well. I want to fish myself—not guide. I'm tired and grumbly and have a PM aspirin hangover. And this girl is just so darn chatty, alive, happy even, for God's sake. But as we descend into the gorge, a canyon wren whistles its ever-decreasing song over the dull roar of the white river below. The smells, sights, and sounds start to overpower my negativity. Just before we reach the bottom I even start to tell Colleen about an osprey that I had seen there the week before; and then the bird appears, as if on cue, and completes the tale for me by diving into the river and catching a fish. Could it be a lucky day? It is a warmish late-October day, just before a predicted storm, and big fish seem to go on the feed before weather hits at that time of year.

But when we reach the river things don't start out so well, as Colleen has been unwise in her selection of footwear and slides down a boulder in her clumsy rubber hippers, busting the reel loose from the rod and screwing up the reel seat. I ruin a pair of pliers trying to bend things back in order. We end up lashing the reel onto the rod with Band-Aids. I then make a most ungraceful entrance into the river and proceed to break off a big rainbow on my first cast. We decide to start over and move upriver a ways. On the way I warn Colleen about a trick rock that is about two feet in diameter and round as a ball. It lives somewhere in the area and is disguised as a normal rock. I landed on it while boulder hopping the year before and it let loose, sending me down very hard.

Colleen takes one side of the river and I the other. She is shy about me seeing her fish, so she moves up out of sight. But it isn't long before I see the glint of a bent fly rod waving around above the boulders. I fish up toward her quickly to see what she has on and watch her land a sixteen-inch brown. And she says that she has caught two more besides. Hell, I don't have to worry about her—that's more than I've caught.

She doesn't mind me watching her fish now that she has proved herself. Which, she has told me, is like what occurs with male customers in the fly shop she works in: she is always having to prove herself because all the guys think that a gal doesn't know much about the sport. But it sure looks like she knows what she is doing—making the short, snappy casts that usually mark a good fly fisher. She says that what she lacks is experience slugging it out with big fish on the Rio. There's no instruction for that; only the fish and the river can teach you that lesson. I suggest a cast into a spot where two moderate currents come together. Her fly drifts down the foam line, and instantly after she sets the hook her rod slams down toward the water, the reel screeches a short shrill song, and then . . . nothing. She turns to me with her mouth and eyes all big and round and can only mutter, "Wow, what was that?" The next big fish slot she fishes produces a similar explosion, but this time Colleen fights the big rainbow more conservatively, so that it doesn't break off. The fish takes advantage of her leniency and runs under a rock, snapping off another fly.

In between all this excitement I'm busy losing my own fish. They are so healthy—so deep and long—that when they get in the wild currents of the river they GO. It is one thing fighting a three- or four-pound trout in calm water, but when they get the raging current of the Rio with 'em, they become even heavier. And it's so difficult to follow them downriver in the tangle of boulders. I have moved into position to fish a very fast run that has just a wee bit of slack water running down the center of it. I cast the nymph up there, and on its way back to me a rainbow over twenty inches grabs the fly. He rips off downstream and I need to follow him, but there is a big rock in the way. While trying to keep the line tight—but not so tight that he wants to run farther away—I somehow

Colleen Treter is joyous at finding a secret fly.

slide up the rock, slip down the other side into water of an unknown depth (which turns out to be waist deep), and continue the fight. But the weight of the fish is just too much in the heavy flow, and the hook pulls out.

I slither over the rock again, take a few deep breaths, and make another cast into that fast run. I wasn't really expecting there to be two hogs in there, so I'm mighty surprised when I hook another fish just slightly shorter than the first. It instantly makes a long greyhounding leap not ten feet in front of me. But it seems to accomplish only half the jump as its great girth pulls it back into the water with a belly flop. And then, wouldn't you know, the rascal makes the same trip downstream as the other fish did, and I have to crawl over the big slimy rock again. Having now gained some experience in the area, I do manage to land this one, but the rest of the big fish I hooked that day are lost.

When I catch up with Colleen, I discover that she has had about the same luck. Plenty of smaller fish, but the bruisers are escaping. But she's had a good day. She was even successful with the all-important "lunch toss." (Remember, she's on one side of the deep river and I'm on the other, and she's got the bread and cheese and I've got the meat and . . . you get the picture.) As we are fixing to fight our way back through one of my famous shortcuts—a maze of boulders, thorns, and vines—I suggest one more spot. She's serious this time. We discuss the lay of the possible battleground and the best places to land a monster fish. She places her pack out of the way, uses just the right amount of line to avoid tangles. She steps up to the plate with a look in her eye like Mark McGuire might have. Sure enough, Gorilla Monsoon grabs the fly and starts ripping around the river. I gave her a little big-fish-fightin' instruction beforehand and she now moves her rod from side to side (instead of holding the weak straight-up position) to tire and steer the fish. We get this savior of a fish safely ashore and congratulate all involved.

Now if the poor girl wasn't beat up enough by the day—her fall at the beginning, hippers filled with water, and a host of other bruises and scrapes (not to mention too loudly my "shortcut"), she receives one more serious blow before getting out of the canyon. As we are walking back along the river—if you can call any travel along that hellhole walking—I turn to say something to her and she raises her head sharply to hear. Unfortunately she is under the overhang of a particularly hard boulder at the time and beans herself sharply. Man, do her eyes ever roll around in her head! She is seeing so many stars that I can see them too.

I get nervous about the whole thing when she starts yawning and wants to "take a little nap." I've never been with anyone who had bumped their yawner before and don't know what to do. But she does, and just goes on her way—and she has the courtesy to compliment me on my attire (I had taken off my waders for the hike up), saying that the plaid shorts I had on over ratty long johns made a good look for me. We tromp up the canyon and off to Questa for a burrito without further incident.

The spectacle known as Colleen remains alive and feisty to this day and is someplace in the high Colorado, no doubt fighting big fish as we speak.

Wild Rivers, upper Rio Grande

Chapter Eight

THE SIDE LESS FISHED

■ ■ ■

I awake at 4:30 a.m. with Mr. Responsibility yelling in a corner of my brain, "We need money! There are bills, calls, emails, and who-knows-what to attend to." But fortunately the turmoil has awakened the Inner Fisherman, who, after sniffing the air, instinctively retorts, "It's cool and damp . . . and being mid-August, the Rio might be really good on such a day. . . . It's been muddy all summer . . . has just cleared . . . and the fish will be all dumbed up since nobody has bothered them . . . and the bills aren't due for a few days." "What a load of crap!" says Mr. Responsibility. "But fishing is our line of work," Inner Fisherman replies without conviction. "I've got to see if the Rio is fishing well, so my guides can take their trips there this week." Mr. R goes straight for the guilt button, saying, "You always choose the fishing—that's why we've never made any money."

Another committee member enters the fray: the Writer. He's the clever one, and winking at the fisherman, says, "Let's take a tape recorder and report the day. Mr. R, you know what a great story that could make. We can sell it for big bucks!" The fisherman and the writer see their window of opportunity and gang up on Mr. R while he is slightly befuddled: "You know that if we are waking up in the middle of the night worrying about details, it must be time to go fishing! When we get back we will get more work done in the long run." Even a dark shadow like Mr. R sees the rationality of that, and my tired body is instructed to start making coffee. Once action is commenced, the committee takes a well-deserved break.

I find myself on the rim of the canyon by 7 a.m., torn up by internal struggle and lack of sleep. There is nobody about, just a piñon jay who yaks with an irritating voice that sounds like one of the committee. The prospect of chasing big fish starts to quiet this overactive noggin, but my mind decides it has one more stop to make before it goes fishing, and it wanders back to the last time I was here alone—it was a year ago, and a low day indeed. I had just dropped my girlfriend, Sandra, off at the Taos airport, where we had had a desperate farewell.

We had been torn apart by the laws of the land, as her visa had expired and she was forced to return to her mother's farm in Patagonia. We had almost married just a week before, but she had changed her mind, and I went from the prospect of spending the rest of my life with her to the prospect of never seeing her again in just a matter of days. I came straight here after her plane went over the horizon because I needed a space as big and lonely as the pain. I wanted to face the worst of it right off and get over her ASAP. And this was the place to do that, because this was where we had camped and fished for "the big"—where our laughter bubbled along the falling water.

I'm remembering how my cell phone surprisingly rang (it doesn't usually work here) and I knew it was her—calling from the Albuquerque airport, crying and promising to return. But I knew better. She wanted to have children and I had already had mine. Here was a gal taught by the gauchos to keep worms in her mouth so that they would be warm for the trout to eat. How's an old fisherman gonna do better than that? I had hiked into the canyon with my chest caved in—feeling as if I had already gotten about as much out of this life as I was going to.

But that was last year, and submitting to the heartache seemed to have gotten me through the grief pretty well. So the memories of Sandra fade as my preparations get me closer to the action. Actually, I've guided dozens of trips this summer and am surprised at my outright enthusiasm. But those days were pretty boring, as I was usually taking beginners after pipsqueak trout—and the fish of the wild Rio Grande are a whole 'nother animal.

I toss deer jerky, cheese, olives, and crackers in the pack, but not much water, because it rained last night and there'll be some in the hollowed-out depressions in the basalt. I put on sunblock, button up, and hide the keys under a bush. The excitement awakens another committee member, the boyish rogue who wants to dash down the trail. But saner heads prevail, and I begin the 700-foot descent at a pace that befits my age.

The roar of the rapids grows stronger as I drop into the box. The view up-canyon is a dramatic blend of angles and bends; the river makes a huge S curve as it crashes through jumbles of basalt. That rock has sloughed off cliffs that rise up in shelves until meeting the forested plane above. Bright green stands of cottonwoods mark several springs here and there. Above the canyon a pyramid-shaped volcano stands in opposition to the V of the gorge, its sharp angles highlighted against the much older and rounder Pot Mountain.

The splendor slows me up, and I lean against a ponderosa to watch how it all sits there. I press my nose to the yellow bark and take a deep whiff of vanilla, then I reach down and grab some of the ever-present sage and rub it over my face. I pick my teeth with a dried ponderosa needle and, proceeding to a juniper, snatch a couple of berries and pop them into my mouth—thus completing the toiletries I neglected in my haste at home.

I reach the water, and while tying two flies on I see several gigantic carp feeding like trout up near the surface. This is unusual; they seem to be eating insects, and they normally grub for moss on the bottom. These big fish are often mistaken for brown trout, and this is probably where the stories of ten-pound browns in the Rio Grande originated. This mystery is maintained because fishermen seldom get to identify these fish because the carp are very difficult to catch. There are ten-pound browns in the Rio, but they are few and far between, live in the long, slow pools, are perhaps nocturnal feeders, and live solely on fish. I cast to one of the carp and they all magically disappear. A wily fish indeed.

Wild-strain Rio Grande cutbow

The river is low, so I cross to the side less fished. The first pool is tricky because it requires a long cast and then some fancy mending. I make a few casts, but I'm not getting that good a drift and decide to try to get closer. I'm wading wet—there isn't much concern about falling in as I'm already "in"—but I carefully maneuver through some submerged rocks on my way to a sandbar in the middle of the pool. Finally I'm in position and make a short cast in a little side current and hook a rotund twelve-inch rainbow.

I then fish out into the main flow, and thinking there might be fish below me, reach my arm way out at the very end of the drift to get another foot of float. The big dry fly makes a slight hesitation, telling me that somebody is fooling with the submerged fly, and I set the hook into a fifteen-incher. It tears up the pool with some acrobatic maneuvers, but I soon have it wiggling in the net. The fight no doubt spooked the area, so now I concentrate on the head of the pool. Any fish there will not have noticed the turmoil below, and this is where the biggest and baddest trout may be found, fish who demand first choice in the chow line. Sure enough, Gorilla Monsoon takes on the first cast and instantly leaps out of the water. It belly flops back in the drink, and I see that it is a beautiful specimen with red sides and pink fins. Like most big fish that live in a large pool, it is hesitant to leave and doesn't try and run off downstream. I'm thankful for that, because it was a chore getting here, and if I had to go back in a hurry I'd be swimming through those rocks that I had just navigated. But after a couple of jumps the fish takes a stand on the bottom and for a moment I think the line is stuck. I keep the pressure on and I am soon admiring four pounds of wild trout—ha!

Fishing has been aptly described as an endless series of opportunities for hope. That's all well, good, and zenful, but hungry fish create more opportunities, thereby causing hope to escalate into anticipation. And I know action is pending in the next pool. It is a small space, and any fish hooked will run to the broken water below. So when I hook some hefty fellow he heads straight downstream and wraps me round a rock. And it's over in the time it took you to read about it—classic encounter for the Rio.

The next place is the far side of a big boulder. It is a great spot, but you can't see your fly when it goes around the rock. I'm usually with a client and get into position so that I can see the fly when it disappears from his view and tell my fisherman when to strike. Solo I can't see the fly, but a second or two after it goes out of sight I just set the hook for the hell of it. I guess I am a bit low on anticipation at that particular moment and not prepared for such a heavy fish, because I come up against such resistance that the rod springs out of my hands and clatters down the great black stone I'm standing on. When I make a move to get it my screwy left leg tweaks, my spiked shoes slip on the slick rock, and I end up straddling the boulder. I shriek. It hurts so much that when the fog lifts, stars appear.

I realize that nothing is broken, but I have severely stretched the inside of my thigh. I reach over behind me and get hold of the rod. When I pull it up tight, the fish is there and starts running off downriver. I try to get up but can't, and in disgust clamp down on the line and just break it.

My left knee had failed because of a previous injury that the canyon was responsible for—after a vigorous day down here, the little muscle above the knee simply popped in half. It sounded like a bone breaking. I also took a doozy of a fall above Arsenic Springs and did something to my shoulder and can't sleep on that side. I've had so many injuries from *Dancing on the Stones*—as John Nichols titled a book about fishing the Rio—that I even had one that was beneficial. I had a weird growth on my elbow for a couple of years, and one day while gracefully flinging myself from rock to rock I landed on one that rolled and I came down so hard on that elbow that it knocked me out cold. The cushion of the growth probably saved me from a broken arm, and the lump busted up and dissipated within a few days.

I'm ready to limp out of there now, but as I am making it toward the trail I come upon a pool that always holds a big fish. But it is a bad place to get at because the river tumbles under a gang of boulders that look like a pile of wrecked SUVs. With my injuries I decide to pass and then wonder if this is a "getting old" compromise. So I ask myself: without the injuries, would I have gone for it? I rationalize that getting old is fraught with good judgment and inner youth says, "Yeah, that's getting old all right."

I head for the trail. When I get there, I take my customary swim to lower the body temperature to make the climb easier. After the swim, I take a drink from a nearby spring and then lie on a little sand beach that is surrounded by tall grass. Several big yellow monarch butterflies sail by. When I attempt to get up, my leg and shoulder protest with shots of pain, so I rest for a bit more before I start up.

Unfortunately, the slow pace forced upon me allows the committee to commence again—they haven't been heard from in several hours and I wonder who this new voice is. Somebody who seems somehow associated with pain, who implies that I might not have much future left down here in this canyon. It's a guy that I am going to hear more and more from: the Old Man. He will be an ally to Mr. Responsibility, and I can just about hear Mr. R saying in the middle of the night, "Since you are a fishing guide and writer, there is no money put away, no insurance or retirement. And you'd better not hurt yourself down there, as you are going to have to guide for the rest of your life." The Old Man will follow with, "Yes, maybe we could fish down along the road, where it's safer."

But the Inner Fisherman, the Writer, and the Youth will no doubt drag me down those obscure trails into the box again. So, my fellow fishermen, if you find my rod lying over on the "side less fished," please do two things for me. First, check to see if the line is tight to a fish—maybe a ten-pound brown has drowned me! (Please let it not be a carp.) And then scratch an epitaph into the hated black rock: "Here ends Taylor Streit's last hookup—he was consumed by a big fish, youth, old age, and the nagging of a pain-in-the-ass committee."

This peacock bass is just big enough to weigh.

PART III

SOUTH AMERICA

Chapter Nine

AMONG

■ ■ ■

I can't get it out of my head that yesterday I was knee-deep in snow and now I'm floating over a sea of green near-a-bouts the equator, headed into the Brazilian jungle after peacock bass. What lies ahead—besides a thousand miles of trees and water—is anyone's guess. These frivolous thoughts vanish as our plane is rocked by a wall of rain. As the jungle disappears below, panic takes hold of me. How in the world will they find a minuscule airstrip down there now? The expressions on my companions' faces reflect similar doubt, but the pilot reassures us by thumbing through a flying magazine draped across the wheel.

Ironically, we have a real, live astronaut onboard. He looks content, but that may not mean all that much, because he's just returned from space, and perhaps he is just delighted being this close to the ground. He has some satellite photos of the rivers we are aimed at. Could be most helpful, but we drop him and his map off at another river. The rest of us fly another hour deeper into the jungle.

The airstrips have been getting shorter and funkier, and this last one looks pretty sloppy after the thick rain. The pilots have ceased reading and are now craning their necks as they circle the pasture/landing strip two or three times. I get the uneasy feeling that they are discussing some sort of alternative in Portuguese, but after buzzing a couple of horses off the landing strip/pasture we finally set down—slipping and sliding to a full stop someplace in the Amazon Basin.

My fishing partner Andy and I take a hike through the tiny town etched out of the bush. The last time I was outside for more than five minutes was in the Rocky Mountain winter yesterday, and the air here seems so hot and thick that it is hard to walk through. We drop down to a slippery wooden dock and meet our guide, Altima, a thirty-year-old Brazilian whose mannerisms suggest he can handle taking a couple of Yanks upriver. He quickly sets our boat against the big muddy flow. The half-mile-wide river divides several times in the next couple of hours, until finally we are running full tilt up a narrow, clear river under a canopy of trees. A beam of light falls on a huge, electric-blue morpho butterfly. It crosses the river by bouncing from one shaft of light to another.

We stop at a lagoon adjacent to the main channel. Our guide gives the universal sign known to all serious fly fishers; his little flick of the wrist starts the mad scramble to assemble our gear. Soon we have gaudy flies aloft: yellow, orange, red, white, and blue, all tied with sufficient crystal flash to light up a peacock bass.

Before long I'm taking pictures of some odd fish: the famous piranha introduces himself, teeth clicking. (He will chop two of our fifty-dollar fly lines in half during the week). Something that looks and acts like a freshwater barracuda is caught, and then we capture a rainbow trout with shark teeth. I'd tell you some of their crazy names, but I think our guide was just making them up as he went along. I have heard that there are more species of fish in the Amazon Basin than in the Atlantic Ocean. This is God's proving ground, and he continuously makes up new creatures as he tosses them down at random—seeing if they fly, swim, crawl, fight, or all of the above. If they survive the Amazon, they are on the list.

I get my first look at the peacock bass—a colorful two-pounder looking kinda like a regular bass, but with vivid green and yellow paint—and a red-orange cutthroat. Actually, it's Andy who's hauling them in; just about when my ego starts to surface, I hook a very nice one that I actually see take the fly about eight feet down in the clear water. It heads for a stick, puts a wrap on it, and holds tight. This is when the fifty-pound tippet comes in handy, and I point the rod straight at him and pull. The branch parts from the tree, and the fish not only has to suffer pressure from me but is also dragging the branch along. The five-pounder doesn't elicit any response from the guide, and once the fish is released he takes us farther upriver. We are refreshed as the air whizzes by, and rounding a bend, we surprise a couple of freshwater dolphins. They sink quickly out of sight, but we also see a giant sloth that simply stares as we pass. At the rate it's moving, I suspect it will still be in the same tree when we head back in a week.

At dusk we reach camp. It has been chopped out of the green tangle and is so tight on the bank that you just hop from boat to dinner table. We are met by our hosts, Garrett and Annie VeneKlasen. They mystically appear out of the mist dressed in summer whites, hand us drinks, and then escort us down winding candle-lit paths to our safari-style tents.

Garrett has run these remote camps for many years and is responsible for discovering this excellent fishery. One of his repeat clients told me, "Garrett probably knows more about catching peacocks than anyone, anywhere." Just having a camp here is an accomplishment, as an immense amount of gear and staff must be hauled in via small boats. (If larger craft could reach the place—for example, commercial fishing boats—there would be fewer big peacocks.)

I've been looking forward to dinner because Garrett and Annie have told me about the weird varmints they eat. So I'm not surprised to be eating somebody called a paca. But when dessert arrives I am shocked to hear it is parrot cake. My hearing is poor, and upon questioning it turns out to be the less exotic carrot cake.

We head upriver the next morning, crossing the equator at 8 a.m. It's carelessly marked with a plastic bag tied to a bush. We fish our way from there up in what is perfect weather for this fishing—bright and hot—way hot when you were rolling in snow the day before. At one point we slip into a hidden lagoon crammed full of three- and four-pounders. One after another they attack the fly—I quickly learn that it must be fished very fast. While I'm standing barefoot on the bow of the boat, a much larger fish than the rest suddenly appears very close and just behind the fly. At the sight of this eight-pounder chasing the ten-inch yellow fly my mouth drops and I freeze. Stopping the retrieve causes the fish to lose interest, and it sinks out of sight. Somebody yells to snap me out of my trance, and when I come to, I swing the rod up; as the fly is about to leave the water there's an explosion directly underfoot, and my little pinkies instinctively curl out of the way of the fish's huge mouth.

That first full day of fishing is compromised somewhat when we return to camp to find that some in our group have caught some very large peacocks with conventional tackle. Most of these guys have been here before and they all seem obsessed with size. I am pretty happy with our couple dozen four- and five-pounders—and the one eight-pounder. I don't get this "hog fever" business—until the next day, when I get it myself, and get it bad.

The day starts with some pretty good action, but the fishing slows when a heavy rain begins to fall. I huddle under my raincoat secretly wishing the action would stay bad so I could get out of this weather and back to camp. But Andy has been down here before and "hog fever" won't let him rest; there is little chance of him quitting as he casts nonstop through the driving rain, his huge yellow fly disappearing from sight as it sails under overhanging tree branches. It lands against a log that has fallen from the dark forest above. He hooks what appears to be another of the numerous sticks, and then, with his rod bent double, turns to me and asks, "Is my line moving?" It does seem to be going somewhere, albeit slowly. I study his extremely bent rod, as generally the size of a fish can be conjured by looking at the rod—the less it throbs, the larger the fish. There is no throbbing or wiggling, just pure pull. When our bored guide becomes intense for the first time in the whole trip, I know we have a serious fish on.

Altima backs the boat out into the middle of the lagoon. Andy and the peacock pull against one another as the fish wages a smart fight, with no jumps to tire it out. We finally get a view of it and it is unnerving to see the green humped back of this big male. It circles the boat time after time just out of reach of the net, and finally, when the fish passes the net again, the fly pulls out and zings by my head. Then I turn to see the monster fish suspended free and motionless; and as I realize that it will disappear at any instant, Altima makes a wild sweep with the long-handled net and captures it. We ogle, awe, photograph, and weigh the sixteen-pound beast before setting it free.

Andy seems much relieved, his obsession abated, to the point that he ceases casting for at least a minute. I, however, have instantly acquired hog fever of the worst kind—unrequited. Mercifully the condition only lasts twenty minutes, because soon I'm trying to convince the guys that I have a fish on, and not a piece of wood, as they suggest. But when my thirteen-pound fish finally takes off, the reel freezes and I look down in horror at fly line wrapped around the reel handle. The only thing I can do is run toward the fleeing fish to loosen the line. Fortunately, I have a boat under me throughout the trip, but I have gear and crew to hurdle. I make the dash from stem to stern in record time. The maneuver gives me enough slack to free the line from the reel and the big bass is off into the backing. The rest of the fight lacks drama in comparison, but now that I am overpowered by hog fever, I want to get rid of this lowly thirteen-pound fish and get my fly out there for a real monster!

Back in camp that evening we find that we have done about as well as fellows fishing woodchopper lures that day. (This woodchopper needs some explanation: it is a very long surface lure equipped with propellers on each end. When the lure is screaming across the surface, all fish in perhaps a one-hectare area think some insane creature has been foolish enough to try and swim across an Amazonian river. This, of course, sends out the law-of-the-jungle signal: eat me now—before the caimans, anaconda, or jaguar do.)

At dinner we learn that a couple of the fellows made an interesting discovery while fishing way upriver in a remote area. They had come across a fisherman's camp that seemed to have been vacated instantaneously: a pot was suspended over a cold fireplace, clothes had been set to dry on a line, and a toothbrush lay beside a cup. No big deal, except the guide figured that the camp had been quit *one year* before. Speculation about the disappearance of the fisherman ran from anaconda to fer-de-lance to jaguar. This, of course, made great dinner conversation, and the possibility of a more mundane explanation was shrugged off. The most popular vision was of a 300-pound "jag" jumping from shadow to firelight, snatching the camper as he stirred his soup. Our host, Garrett, then spiced the intrigue by telling us a chilling story of an anaconda attack in the vicinity the previous year.

The anaconda, although docile on land, is deadly and cunning in its watery element, planning an attack and then lying in wait for its victim. One of the campers almost fell prey, as he was in the habit of bathing at a certain place, at a certain time, and a very large snake slung a wrap on him and started hauling him out into the river. He managed to grab onto a tree and gave—I'm sure—a most spirited yell. Rescuers arrived and beat the twenty-some-foot snake off.

The caimans also give us considerable sport. After cocktails one evening (caiman wrestling seems to peak just after happy hour) we take a moonlight cruise with a spotlight to find just the right croc for wrestling. After passing up dozens with too much space between their shining yellow eyes (big ones), we volunteer our most inebriated member (Andy) to leap from the boat at one just bigger than a frog. Unfortunately, it turns out to be as slippery as a frog too, and it escapes.

The serious caiman adventure happens back in our cozy camp the next night. After a fine dinner that includes more jungle fare, stories naturally turn to hunting lions in Africa, fighting huge catfish (part of the night's repast), and other such chitchat. This is interrupted by word from one of the hands that a huge caiman has been apprehended just a few feet down the riverbank. You can't keep lion hunters and catfish fishermen away from such an adventure, and we dash off to witness the spectacle—even leaving dessert to do so.

When we get there we are treated to the sight of several workers hauling a four- to five-meter caiman up on the bank by several of the staff. It's being "taught a lesson" by the workers, who have grown tired of it coming so close to camp. The final straw occurred earlier that day when it popped up close to the laundry girl.

The entrails of the very catfish we are digesting were his downfall. They've been attached to a shark hook with plenty of half-inch wire as "shock tippet." It is a wild scene with the fellows pulling on the beast and about a dozen workers, their kids, and as many clients dancing excitedly on the cramped beach. The animal is being dragged toward us, and no one is on the tail side to apply the brakes should Nasty Boy decide to lurch into the crowd. Upon this realization a couple of the non-lion-hunting types climb up a tree, and howls of laughter are heard when a light finds them there. This is high drama and at least a million laughs for everyone, especially the Brazilian men who, after the insanity and boredom of releasing fish for a bunch of silly Yankees, finally have something exciting to do. When the photos have been taken and the hoopla subsides, a frightened and unhappy Nasty Boy is tied to a tree on the tiny peninsula. (It is illegal to kill caiman in Brazil.)

We return to cold dessert and heated debate about Nasty Boy's fate. The lion stalkers want the natives to finish him off—illegal or not. The catch-and-release faction wonders how the brute could be unhooked without bloodshed. I, not having to wash clothes in the river, refrain from comment.

Nasty Boy is alive and kicking the next morning, but underfoot. An excellent compromise is reached. To keep him from devouring anyone, he is to be parked across the river, where he will be out of the way until our departure—giving him some time to think about the price of lusting after the laundry girl.

Not all creatures in this big, wet world are covered with warts and slime. We see beautiful birds daily: gorgeous yellow and blue macaws are always seen in pairs, arguing as they fly. Altima takes great delight in escalating their quarrels, with what must have been some pretty randy macaw talk of his own, for they carry on no end after conversing with him.

Then there is the toucan—from what I can gather from its flight plan, not a quick-witted bird, because it doesn't fly straight, but hops through the air. Or more accurately, it constantly falls down as it flies. It would appear that its huge bill weighs more than its body. And as it goes lazily along, the forward luggage pulls the rest toward earth. Upon realizing its downfall, the stupid bird flaps its wings faster to get back on track. You'd expect that it would figure this out and plan for the downfall, but it goes a few more feet, forgets about the forward luggage again, and as its flapping slows, it sinks once more. And then, more vigorous wing beats raise it back on course.

But let's get back to the fishing, because the next day's angling is extraordinary. Fish eat our flies consistently all day. (Everyone does great that day and the ten clients' total catch is estimated at over 1,500 pounds of fish.) In a tiny cove just off the river's fast water, a downed tree gives us a couple of dozen big bass. We have to put the fly between just the right branches of the fallen tree. Then, when the Teeny 300 line sinks just so, one strip and you're into one. It's like fishing a crappie hole except these guys are four to nine pounds! The incredible fishing goes on until a giant river otter gets wind of the action: when its head pops up close by it marks the end of things.

We generally fish large still-water "lagoons," where we cast toward shore, cruising along under the power of a trolling motor. This is a lot like regular bass fishing—great when you are in a mess of feeding fish, but if they are not eating, it is a lot of work with the ten weight and huge fly. But what all serious fly rodders like best is sight fishing, and we get to do it that day in a clear river that looks like a trout stream.

Stopping for lunch on a pleasant little sandbar on the edge of the fast-flowing narrow river, I abandon my bass sandwich when I see a seven-pound peacock cruising under some branches. I grab the rod and slip down toward him—which comes naturally to me as the water is reminiscent of a small New Mexico trout stream. But overhanging trees make it hard to cast and I try to keep my eye on the fish as I maneuver into position. The big fish drifts in and out of sight as it winds through the shadows. But there is no way to get any kind of cast in there—and the fly isn't doing much good sitting in my right hand. And so, when the fish is so close that I'm afraid that it will see me, I throw the fly into the water. Seven pounds of fish looks real big from less than a rod's length away, as it streaks across the bright sand to swipe at the fly. I feel like I am under attack, too. It takes off out into the stream, but because of the brush I can't raise the rod to set the hook, so when the line gets tight, I slam that hook home. I splash out through the tree branches and fight the fish out in a more open part of the little overgrown stream.

On our way back downriver, we have more sight fishing. We catch fish here and there, but nothing big. In our last spot, however, the river looks very fishy; it widens and falls off a shallow sandbar into a deep hole. On the inside of this bend is a large area of knee-deep water over sand. A deep pool drifts into the jungle on the far side, and Andy heads over in the boat while I wade the flat. Right off I notice schools of the large bait-fish that Garrett had told me the big peacocks love. And sure enough, as soon as I start down these shallows I see a freshwater stingray approach with a six- or seven-pound bass behind it. It rushes the fly and grabs it just like a hungry bonefish would.

I laugh over to Andy, but he is busy with some kind of serious fish on his line and being backed in the open. They tell me in no uncertain terms to get unhooked from that minnow I have on, wade closer, and cast next to his fish. They then describe the fish they have on as fifteen pounds, and another one trying to steal the fly away from him at that very moment as "considerably bigger." By the time I land my "minnow" and get over near the boat, the companion fish is gone, but we get some photos of Andy's great bass.

I am given the bow and off to the hole we go. We can see the hogs down there and maybe, we hope, the boss hog has found his way back. When my fly lands in that tiny cove, fish appear everywhere. And here comes this absolute monster, dwarfing the rest. It closes in on the fly . . . and then a much smaller fish rushes in and grabs it. It turns out to be an almost ten-pound peacock, and I haul them out of there till my arms ache—all the same size as the first and fighting like crazy. I get them in the boat as quickly as possible, because we are running late (being still way upriver) and the camp boat can now be heard coming from downriver to fetch us out of the darkening jungle. Wild-eyed with hog fever, I only want the boss hog peacock, and these eight- and nine-pounders just aren't cutting it! The drone of the camp's outboard gets louder and louder, and then, as the boat pulls beside us, I release the last peacock—and a long, deep breath—and slump into my seat.

Red sun at night, fisherman's delight

CHAPTER TEN

THE FIVE-PESO FLOAT

Part I

■ ■ ■

I paid the bus driver five pesos and got off at Rinconada Bridge. He helped me drag the tiny boat out of the luggage compartment and down to the river. In an hour I had the craft inflated, the camping gear roped in behind, and the flippers firmly attached to my feet.

Trial by fire is my standard MO. I'm not happy doing things that way—it's just this lazy man's way. As I had never floated any sort of river with this wee boat, I was pretty scared when I shoved off into the swift Collon Cura River. The knot of fear in my chest expanded when, after floating only a few feet, I realized that the flippers were a totally inadequate means of steering the tiny catamaran in the strong currents of this huge river. (I'd forgotten to bring the oars along.)

If I was going to turn back, this was the time to do it. . . . better to quit here than downriver, where there was no road? What to do—what to do? Better decide quickly, as the river was sending me on its way. . . . I knew that there weren't any really danger-ous rapids ahead and I guess the pull of the current, and the fish awaiting downriver, were stronger than the evaporating opportunity to turn back. Once I managed to get the awkward vessel in the main flow I grabbed my fly rod and started slinging orange whooly buggers toward the banks. That helped settle me down.

I can't begin to describe all of the trout I caught—that's standard for this river. Rainbows were a dime a dozen. But what I was really after were big browns that should have been moving upriver to spawn. Fish that normally lead solitary, nocturnal lives in deep, dark holes are, for this one time of year (fall), out and about. But it is hard fig-uring out where those spawners will be; they like the tails of pools and small streams,

Author and studly brown trout in Patagonia

but there were no such streams for them to ascend here, so I headed to the smallest in a number of river braids. I searched the fast riffles for water deep enough to hide a big, carnivorous brown. Sure enough, at the first knee-deep spot something latched onto the fly and just sat there. Argentine brown trout feed on a crayfish-type crustacean called a pancora, and they get so rotund on this plentiful food that pulling one in is like hauling in an anchor. But a lot of side pressure moved him, and it wasn't long before I was unhooking a four-pound brown. Its color proved that it was in the spawn: bright red and brown spots were dabbed over a dull yellow background, which faded to reddish orange along the fins and belly.

I stripped the flies across another channel and got blasted by one rainbow after another. One highly motivated eighteen-incher tried to escape capture by leaping onshore. He flew over the branch of a tree and broke off. I decided to look somewhere else for browns. The size of the rainbows was a predictable two to three pounds, but with the browns, who knew how big they'd get?

I would have spent more time on my mission, but the sun was waning behind some nasty-looking clouds that towered over the Andes. The wild formation looked like a fleet of steel-gray spaceships stacked on top of each other and signaled that the famous Patagonian wind would be howling down from the mountains soon.

I set up camp on the lee side of a thick clump of willows. Keeping with the spirit of the trip, I threw a considerable hunk of Argentine range beef right on the fire (I'd forgotten the grill). The wind arrived in time to flavor the meat with ash and sand—and a smattering of moisture. I choked down the meal and quickly erected a small tarp to try and stay dry (I'd forgotten the tent). But no matter how I tried to tie it down, it flapped so hard that I chose to remove it and suffer the light rain.

If that wasn't bad enough, some odd creature under my bed was making a noise that could best be described as a thumping quack. It was like a frog croaking from hell. I believed it to be a dream for the longest time, but then when I realized that there was a real varmint tormenting me I flew into a fit of insanity and started digging with bare hands. Sand flew everywhere, but when I got the flashlight, there were no devil frogs to be found. The croaking stopped with all that activity, to (of course) resume as soon as I settled back in the sleeping bag. I tried to rectify the matter by moving a few feet, but devil frogs were there too!

I needed plenty of coffee the next morning, but I had forgotten the coffeepot, so I had to hunt through the bushes for a can to heat water in. Once I was sufficiently revved up, I headed on foot up the nearby Chimehuin River—a river well known for big browns. The water wasn't much for the first half mile or so, but I caught a couple of fish. Then I came to a big, deep pool that was created when the river made an abrupt turn against a sheer cliff. I caught a small one right off, but the best water—behind a big boulder sitting midstream—seemed beyond my reach. With the cliff right behind me, all I could do was cast parallel to it and wing a change-of-direction cast at a right angle to the cliff.

After a bunch of tries I finally slung one out behind the big rock. Somebody grabbed it right at the surface. Not much happened for a while as the fish hung in the current. Then it started swimming in circles around the pool and boring down with heavy thrusts. I knew this wasn't your average fish, and I became very anxious to see it. On one of its rounds I put all the muscle I dared into the rod to get a glimpse, but I couldn't raise it. This was like battling a big saltwater fish as its circles got smaller and the fish started coming closer to the surface. When I got a good look at it I almost lost my grip on the rod; but I managed to hold on tight, and the beast finally floundered at the surface. Each time its huge head cleared the water I pried it closer to shore—rod doubled over in agony. Walking slowly backward with steady pressure, I maneuvered the huge brown between some rocks.

My eyes were as big as the spots of the hooked-jawed male as I got down on my knees to worship the monster. It had none of the brightness of the other spawners. This fish had deep brown spots over a silvery background. I can usually tell the length of a trout with a glance but with this fish, I had no idea of its size until I actually laid the tape on it. Twenty-eight and a half inches!

I let it go, and I wish I could show you a picture, but the camera (I'd forgotten the camera) was with the oars, grill, and coffeepot way back upstream, and by now it was all about downstream.

Rainbow over Fingers of God, Limay River, Argentina

CHAPTER ELEVEN

THE FIVE-PESO FLOAT

Part II

■ ■ ■

If you were with me last chapter, you know that I'm floating down some misspelled river in Argentina—accompanied only by the howls and squeals of the famous Patagonian wind. I have just caught the biggest trout of my life, and aside from having forgotten most of the essential gear, I'm having a hearty time of it.

This angry wind seems determined to scour everything—including me—from the earth's surface, and has blown me onshore. I'm forced to walk the boat downriver. I exhaustedly round another bend as a flock of pink flamingos tries to fly into the gale. They give up after flapping in place and simply drop straight back to the riverbank.

I make camp under an embankment, and after clearing a large area of all combustibles very carefully get a fire going. While I'm cooking dinner, a red fox prances by, sees me, and sits down not fifty feet away. The animal hangs around all through dinner before it finally trots off into the twilight. With dark, the wind that has been with me for the last couple of days finally quiets. I throw an extra log on the fire and watch the flames go peacefully up instead of sideways.

I can hear myself think again, and I reflect on how a trip like this clears the cluttered mind and lets one see clearly—perhaps too clearly. So that when you hit civilization you see what is really going down—a brutal shock to a person who has been tenderized by the great powers of nature. Maybe it's better to just stay home and forever trudge through the prescribed reality so you don't have such a descent. As I sit there watching the fire I grow depressed realizing I'm about to reach the road tomorrow. It isn't too bad to come out of this wilderness into an Argentine town. But I'm heading back to the States in a couple days, and I know the sock in the jaw is coming. Experience has taught me that when my plane touches down in pagan Miami I'll stiffen up in anticipation of the collective anger that waits. It never fails to depress me, because I know I will inevitably join in the melee too. Porters swear and yell, businessmen harass each other on cell phones, impatient mothers shame their kids in public (something you never see in Argentina). I think back to last year's arrival in the States.

I had met an Argentine woman on the plane who was excited about her first trip to my country. I saw her again in the airport and she asked me to help her get some film. We found some at a thin crevice of a store tended by a wide and toothless woman. She was so rude that the Argentine woman walked away with her hand pressing on her chest (that powerful feminine gesture that contains shock and pain). She had stepped, innocently, from a land where people don't treat each other that way. Argentines are prone to smile, embrace, and talk—endlessly—leaving her ill prepared for our curt interchanges. This is the USA and humanity isn't cost effective.

I'll expect to be overwhelmed by the money and all the gear, too. One person to every new car, a TV in every pot, efficiency from top to bottom, right to left—it's a nice machine to visit, but living inside it?

But stifle yourself, poundmeister, all isn't so gloomy, you've got one more day on the river. And a beautiful day it is, too: marshmallow clouds sail on a light breeze and

The McCloud River rainbow was introduced to Argentina a hundred years ago.

I'm able to float in peace for a change. Too perfect to fish very hard—and I decide to use only dries. I make a cast here and there because I happen to have a rod in my hand, but the sway of the willows and the bright humor of the water keep me entertained. I'm not thinking about fishing—until I actually see some fish rising, that is. I park the boat below them and sneak up low, as they are along the bank and might spook. I trick a couple of one-kilo fish—one of which almost climbs on the bank to eat the dry. (There are no raccoons, bears, eagles, or osprey in Patagonia to threaten the trout, so they are often found in exposed places.)

Speaking of birds, there are all kinds of the delightful creatures flitting and sailing about. I have considerable history with the birds of Patagonia from hanging out with Lorenzo Sympson. Lorenzo oversees a couple of condor studies that happen to overlap my fishing, and he has helped me out by lodging, feeding, and entertaining many of my clients. We floated this piece of river together once, and he pointed out a high rock face that the condors use. When I drifted by it yesterday there were condors flying out from the cliffs. He had told me that the huge birds use the cliffs for shelter during stormy

The European red deer was also introduced to Argentina.

weather but never nest there. The birds that use the place are from the Traful river clan, which is about seventy-five miles away. That's just a short flight for these huge birds as they travel great distances to find food. When they find it they signal by flashing the white patches on the tops of their wings. Then the next condor relays the "come and get it" signal to the next relative on down the line, until they are grouped together. Then they descend to the food. With the addition of cattle and red deer to Patagonia there are more condors now than ever.

Condors prefer higher elevations and seldom come down by the rivers, but many bird species live near the water in this parched landscape. The little negrita flits its orange wings as it nervously hops from rock to rock. Tero teros run and bob and then make obnoxious calls when you get anywhere near them. The rasping croak of the bandurria sounds like something out of a science fiction movie. There are many ducks and geese with perhaps the most common being the spectacle duck—some of which fly very close by my boat. Delicious dove and quail abound and although I miss several with rocks I do successfully practice-shoot several with the fly rod.

On such a still day, the roaring of the red stag is everywhere to be heard. As I'm floating downstream, a great stag herds a group of hinds across a shallow riffle below me. He has a magnificent rack with a crown of three or four points at the top. When he gets them about halfway across, a smaller stag starts to follow the herd, but the big one turns and makes an angry roar that stops the smaller bull. Then the old man makes a bit of a charge toward the smaller stag and that sends it shirking off.

After I watch the deer disappear into the woods, I walk over to fish a slow pool off the main current. These are excellent places to see cruising fish, and I spot a twenty-inch rainbow sailing along leisurely. But when I go to make the cast I smack the rod into a branch and break it near the tip. Since I'm going home tomorrow I can get it fixed then, and I'm having such a pleasant day that I'm not bothered by the incident. The broken rod and the day's mood suggest that it might be time to leave Argentine trout alone for another year.

But somehow I hook a twelve-incher while wading back to the boat. I am reeling it in over my shoulder as I trudge along, when it seems to get much bigger all of a sudden. At first I think that it has swum under something and snagged, but when I turn around I see a brown trout of immense proportions arrogantly holding the twelve-incher crossways in its mouth—not twenty feet away from me! I have fished for forty-five years awaiting this event. It looks like a pit bull off its leash, and my heart leaps into my throat as the horrible fish swims off to the middle of the river with its prize. I think I'll give the great fish time to swallow the not-so-great.

I wait—the rod throbs as Beastie Boy munches, with the broken rod tip hanging by a thread—then set the hook as hard as I dare, hoping that the smaller fish is way down inside the gullet of the great one. Maybe the size-twelve hook will dislodge from the little fish and, in its long journey up from the bowels of the great fish, will stab itself into its throat? I've heard a story of an Argentine trout that simply refused to let go in such a situation and was landed without ever being hooked. But I figure that was a long shot. After I strike I am still fast to the fish, and I don't know if what happens for the next few minutes can be described as a fight—it is more like Beastie Boy casually swimming around with me following behind. He finally wanders up close again—I can clearly see him with the rainbow's tail hanging out of his mouth. As if to show me what he thinks of the whole stinking affair, the great one turns in my direction, opens his mouth, and lets the not-so-great one out.

Maybe I actually feel relieved to be released. I reel the bug-eyed not-so-great in and give him some resuscitation. He swims away, listing a little—imagine having two different species of carnivores pulling at you from opposite ends.

The next day finds me in a bus bound for Buenos Aires. I'll spend two days in the noise and bustle of BA in preparation for reentry into the United States. I'm watching a movie stretched out in a fine Mercedes bus, as a scene of New Mexico flashes by on the screen. I think that at least there is some relief from the States—inside the States. The movie ends and is replaced by a Bach sonata as our stewardess serves tea. Just for practice I look around to see if there are any dangerous-looking scoundrels aboard. Everyone looks OK, and I sit back and sip my tea. Much different from a Trailways bus trip back home.

Chapter Twelve

BY HOOK OR BY CROOK

■ ■ ■

When fly-fishing in Argentina it is not all that uncommon to have a big brown trout chase a smaller fish that you have on the line. It is usually just a brief strafing action and then the big fish is gone. But these skirmishes can escalate, and once on the Chimehuin River I had a brown trout that was perhaps ten pounds eat a twelve-inch rainbow that I was playing. (See The Five-Peso Float—Part II.) I had hoped to hook the large fish with the hook that was already in the mouth of the smaller trout. There was also the off chance that the huge trout was arrogant enough to refuse to release its prey and I might get to land it without actually ever hooking it.

These normally wise predatory browns can become so determined to eat whatever they have latched onto that they lose all sense of caution. On a remote New Mexico river I witnessed a brown trout of eighteen inches try to devour a family member roughly half its length. This was such an opportunistic undertaking for the larger fish that it became incapacitated as it struggled to devour the smaller fish—they tumbled downriver on the whims of the currents as one fish disappeared down the gullet of the other.

One blue day in Patagonia, I dropped off a couple of good clients—one by the handy name of T. J. Trout—on a river with their guide. With a hunk of time to spare, another guide and I decided to explore a roadless little river that had sparked my imagination for years. Seen only from a distance, the shining watercourse seemed to disappear into the Patagonian wasteland. Reaching the stream required wading across another really big river, and Santiago and I linked arms to make the crossing. It took a while, because we went by some nice water and caught a couple of warm-up fish. When we got to the mystery stream, I cast into the first nice pool and hooked an eight-inch rainbow.

Fish vs. fish—Brownie attempts ass-backward apprehension of Baby Trucha.

As I was bringing in the "nuisance fish," a male brown of just of about four pounds sped out of a submerged root pile and started after the rainbow. As stated earlier, this has happened enough throughout my decades of fly-fishing that I didn't get unraveled and let the line loose to see what would happen—which was an easy guess: the brown trout tried to grab the little rainbow. But the little trout was a slippery fellow, and Brownie lost his grip and the little fish swam away. Brownie was turning this way and that looking for it, and I pulled the well-hooked baby trout into the other fish's sights. Brownie again attacked Baby Trucha, but the little bow again got free. Brownie just wasn't getting much of a handle on the little one, and this happened over and over. I was trying to help and would lift Baby Trucha out of the water and plop it back on Brownie's head. The splat of the trout on Brownie's head didn't seem to spook the wise old carnivore, who was by now so totally obsessed with acquiring Baby Trucha that I decided to see just how far this could be taken.

But I should set the scene a little better. I was on the bank, standing upright in full view—there were no background bushes or trees to cover me, and the river bottom sloped gradually away. I started luring Brownie into the shallow water with what by now was a rather spent Baby Trucha. Just as the old guy's mouth would be about to close

Santiago "Sancho" Ramis holds one by hook—
and one by the crook.

on the feast, I'd pull the little fish toward shore. I continued doing this until Baby was in such shallow water that the larger fish's back was out of the water! And mind you, this was only a rod's length away and I was making no attempt to disguise myself.

The big fish finally backed out a few feet. About this time Santiago approached and I excitedly waved him over. As he neared, I was taking pictures of the interesting positions that Brownie and Baby Trucha assumed. In fact at one point Brownie tried to swallow Baby T ass-backward-tail-first.

Santiago was as amazed as I by this outlandish fish behavior. After I showed him a few of the tricks that the two fish could do, we decided to try and land the big brown by teasing it to shore—as I had already done. So I let Brownie get about half of Baby T in his mouth and then pulled him up to us, where Santiago lifted him up tail first—by the "crook" (see photo), as we call it in the fishing trade. We took some photos and then set the pair free. I was tempted to see if Brownie would still try to eat Baby Trucha after this, but we just let the two fish wander off without further interference from us bothersome humans.

Lone fisherman in the Andes

CHAPTER THIRTEEN

ARGENTINE LAKES

■ ■ ■

As storms sweep eastward off the southern Pacific, they deposit generous amounts of rain and snow over the Andes. Although most of this precipitation falls in Chile, much of the water actually ends up in Argentina—by way of small streams that pour into huge natural lakes that lie just inside Argentina. Great rivers then emerge from these lakes to flow into the Atlantic hundreds of miles to the east.

As the outlets (bocas) of these lakes draw huge fish, the fisherman is found not far behind. But the lakes themselves receive only light fishing pressure because most people prefer river fishing. And the lakes are usually so remote and windswept that accessing them may require long drives, hikes, or boat rides. Few North Americans on weeklong vacations care to go to all that trouble.

Lago Tromen, Argentina

But these lakes nestle idyllically in the lonely mountains, and so overpowering is the view of the surrounding forest that the fly fisher may have trouble keeping his attention on the fishing. Bright emerald reeds parallel the shore and give way to branches that sweep down from magnificently tall trees. Big trout cruise amid all this foliage.

And if you are fortunate enough to spend the night lakeside, you will find that camping in the Argentine is very agreeable: there are few bugs or people, no snakes, and jets don't trail overhead. Add the succulent aroma of meat roasting over the parilla and you will think that you have died and gone to trout bum heaven.

Chapter Fourteen

THE ROYAL BROOKIE

■ ■ ■

To most fly fishers, brook trout are just pretty little fish that don't take dry flies, fight, jump, or even think. But by some mysterious law of attraction I became a hopeless brookie addict, being seduced at a tender age by their orange, white, and black fins waving in the currents of the Catskill Mountains' little streams. I'd slither streamside looking for a big brookie—somebody over nine inches. One that went into double figures was memorable and twelve inches was historical.

In more recent decades, those standards stretched with my horizons, making my twenty-inch goal a little too challenging to be attained within the continental United States. As time goes by, real life has a way of pushing aside such silly notions—well, most of them, anyway—and when I started fishing Argentina the old obsession resurfaced.

My first encounter with fontinales in the Argentine was with my friend Pedro, at a nameless lake in the Andes. We headed to the far end dragging a boat down a shadowed road. After we had laid some logs down to repair a primitive bridge, Pedro whispered that we were in the demilitarized zone between Argentina and Chile, and that Pablo Neruda escaped Chile on this poetic course. When we finally got to the secret spot, I knew we were in big brookie territory when Pedro apologized for the first fish, as it was only a little fifteen-incher! "There are big ones, too!" he said. We caught some where a creek came into the lake and then found a pool up that creek surrounded by jungle that had a bunch, but none that reached my magical twenty-inch mark.

Years later at Lago Falk we found a school of the slumbering fish that we could easily see in the ultra-clear water twenty feet below us. We hooked one or two with sinking lines by stripping the fly by the fish. My son, Nick, got one that was over

Kingfisher and Lanin Volcano

eighteen inches. When we had caught all we were going to that way, we hung the muddlers off of floating lines and way-long tippets. The lethargic fish were much more interested in the nonswimming fly than in a retrieved one, it turned out (probably because that fly acted more like their chief food, snails—and, as we all know, snails don't move very fast).

One fish was clearly the leader of the pack. I maneuvered the fly in front of his nose, and after a few seconds he swam over and sucked it down. When I saw the white of his mouth I set the hook. After a lot of tugging on both our parts, the fish was boatside. Nick got it into the boat and held it up for us to photograph and measure, but it made a wiggle and shot out of his hand and landed back in the drink. An accident? I think not. Hadn't Nick just caught the biggest brookie of his life and, as per usual, wasn't he instantaneously usurped by numero uno? Our companion Arturo did manage a quick photo, but he and I have "issues," and when he took his camera for a swim that evening in the Rio Manso I was sure that foul play was afoot. Sure enough, when we developed his film, there was no brookie. (The truth is I don't think it was twenty inches anyway—maybe nineteen.)

Surely I have made my point: to me, the brook trout is the king of trout and the blue blood of all fishes. And it acts just like royalty as it prances around in gaudy dress and lounges about in incestuous schools. So on the day that I finally captured my twenty-inch brookie, it was fitting that I had the honor to fish for royalty—with royalty.

I was tagging along on a guide trip with my associates in Patagonia, Angel and Gabe, to fish some water I'd never seen. We picked the clients up in a van, and I was sitting way in the back. When I was first introduced to them, I instantly knew that I was not fishing with the regular gang of crude sportsters I'm used to. Their quality was apparent when I was offered their delicate hands for the kissing! I was then formally informed that I was going to be spending the day with a Russian countess and another titled aristocrat of some other great European nation—I forget which.

The relative of a very famous and privileged person provided this information to me, and although ignorant of the hierarchy of titles—whether a duke is ranked over duchess or a count presides over a lord—I could only imagine the status of the introducees with such a formidable introducer! I'm not sure if his blood was of a royal blend, but considering his status in the group, lofty nature, and prestigious fishing qualifications, we will refer to him from here on as "the King."

I should add that it took a few minutes for me to learn all this, because he tried several languages on me before he hit on mine—American. These folks moved from language to language with ease—all except for the Russian countess and me. Judging by the elegance of her bearing I don't think she ever needed to explain herself beyond her capacity. And I, of course, as an American, expect people to learn to speak American if they are in a continent that has the word America in it. Especially someplace called *South* America.

We had an hour's drive to the lake, and the van quickly filled with smoke; this was Argentina, where most people smoke cigarettes, but royalty puff pipes to raise their allure above that of the commoners. How else are they going to announce their station? It wouldn't do to wear a crown or robes to fish, and you would have never known they were titled by their fishing gear—they weren't exactly in tatters, but tatters edged some of their apparel. All that was well disguised, however, by the generous silk scarf-age that bubbled from their necks. An embarrassing amount of fiberglass was used in the construction of their fly rods.

But when the pipes were removed, a great deal of jocularity ensued from the group members' mouths—all except for the fourth and trailing member of the entourage, who, when we had reached the lake, dragged up behind his companions like the hunchback of Notre Dame. He was the King's brother and a very large and frightening man with a slanting gait that elevated one shoulder. This cocked his head, but his knit black hat was worn on the level—thereby putting one eye, and one lens of his thick glasses, underneath the hat. His speech was a low mumble that oozed out of the high side of his mouth.

I later asked Gabe if these folks were of such outstanding pedigree, and he informed me that they were indeed, and, as he put it, they were "happy about that." As I was soon to find out, the King was indeed a fisherman of the first order. He told me that he had fished in sixty-three different countries and sailed all the seas in search of the billfishes. I countered this with "I wrote two books on fly-fishing"; he slapped me back with the fact that he had written fourteen. He had also owned the largest fly shop in Rome. This put me on a pecking order somewhere behind his brother, and I went and hid in the little cabin in the boat, keeping my mouth shut until Gabe and I were dropped off to fish.

The place was only accessible by boat and rarely fished. The trout were so slow witted that you could fish for them by gently motoring along looking for rising and cruising fish, then tossing a big dry near them and popping it like a bass bug. This type of fishing is far more royalty-friendly than the vigorous exploring mission Gabe and I had planned. So we were let off at a boca as the royal carriage continued down the coast. The boca was formed where a good-sized river entered the lake; the river was a rough and tumbling affair but slowed and fanned out into several currents to get on equal terms with the lake. There were drop-offs, eddies, sunken logs, and a pair of black-neck swans feeding on aquatic vegetation nearby. To further beautify the scene, a forest of great trees stood against the blue-white glaciers of the towering Lanin Volcano—nearly 10,000 feet over the lake.

I started fishing the boca with a Teeny 130. Gabe warned me to be on the lookout for fish as I waded out to where the strongest current fell over a shelf that had eddies revolving on each side. I made casts in the shallow water while wading out, but nothing showed. When I got within reach of the hot spot, I cast across the current, let the line sink, and then retrieved so that the fly would swing just under the drop-off. I tried the place for fifteen minutes or so, but nada. Gabe was fishing the shallow water right where a channel of the river came in, and he raised a big bow to a dry. He said that its mouth came up out of the water and yawned so wide that he struck too soon. He then had me move between two currents, where logs crisscrossed the bottom. There would be a lot of lost flies in such a spot, but it was where he suspected the neighborhood school of brookies would be.

On about my third cast I latched onto something that sure felt like a big brookie—or a tree branch that swam. When it turned underwater there was a length of brookie red that looked to span that elusive twenty-inch mark. It pulled hard for a time, but I let it do its struggling out beyond the logs, and when it had tired I steered it in between those obstructions and slid it onto shore. What a feeling of relief to see such a fish lying there! I said to Gabe that it sure looked like a twenty-incher, and he said it was big. Gabe took the official measurement at exactly twenty inches, and photos were taken. Gabe, who hadn't grown up hunting these fish in their native habitat

My twenty-inch brookie finally comes ashore!

like I did, and hadn't developed the same obsession, nonchalantly mentioned that he had caught even bigger ones here. But that didn't confront me, and I was plenty happy watching my prize swim away.

Like a lot of things longed for during the course of life, when they are finally attained—what was the big deal? And since there were more fish to be caught, no doubt, I decided not to wait for word from on high that I had reached some new level of enlightenment by catching a fish, and went to the next channel and took "little" brookies (they had now all become "little") till I tired of it. While I was so employed, Gabe caught several rainbows, all over twenty inches, by popping Chernobyl ants on the edge of a couple of eddies.

But our big exploration of the day was to be up the river. If anyone should find their way here, the brush, boulders, and strong currents would likely turn them back to all that marvelous—and easy—fishing waiting at the boca. But we have some pretty hardy clients from time to time who are looking for new thrills, and we wondered if it would be worth bringing them here. It was a striking place, as boiling white water seemed to explode out from the dark forest.

I moved upriver as Gabe fished the first pool above the boca. His shaded figure was highlighted against the lake, and I watched his rod suddenly bend and saw him fight a nice fish there. I waited for him to catch up, and when he did, we fished up the wild river, he forcing his way up one side and me the other. We both flung dry/dropper into all the pockets. But even though we were covering a lot of water we weren't catching anything. And we fished a halfmile before we finally caught a minnow of a rainbow. But just when I yelled over to Gabe that we should probably be fishing this cold river in midsummer rather than fall, I got a strike on the dry. I missed the fish, but it made a bigger splash than a baby trout would. I sent the fly back in there several times and it finally hit the dry again. I was surprised to pull up tight to a very heavy fish. I got a glance at this nice brown as it motored past me, gathering strength as the white water helped propel it downriver. But I was fishing 3X, and by racing downstream adjacent to the brute we managed to have it in hand quickly. It measured out at twenty-one inches.

From there up we encountered only small fish, so we decided to take a trail upriver that Gabe and his girlfriend had cut out of the bamboo in the spring. He told me that there were miles of water ahead that never got fished. Once we got up on the steep slope to the ridge above the river, we walked

Fuchsia

for a half mile but then had a hard time finding a way back down to the water. We'd passed a great-looking pool and decided to turn around and try to get to it. We slipped and slid down the steep slope, grabbing the bamboo to slow the fall.

Gabe generously had me start fishing this enchanted pool, formed where the river flung itself into a huge rock. Green moss covered the rock, and bright red fuchsia grew from it. The flowers were occasionally caught by little wavelets; the mix of colors would then drip back into the sparkling river. All this was illuminated by dabs of light that filtered through the swaying trees high above. An even prettier sight appeared when one of the beams of light played over a long rainbow trout finning below the great rock. I put several casts in front of him with no luck; but he was holding rather deep, so I put a heavier bead head poundmeister nymph on. When it got down to the fish's zone the big bow ate it; we measured this one at twenty-two and then went up toward the head of the pool.

After Gabe had fished it with the dry/dropper I put the Teeny line on to see what would happen with a streamer deep. In Argentina the brown trout eat a completely different diet than the rainbows, so you can fish a piece of water in one fashion for rainbows, and then fish it again another way. I sent my bead head copper muddler in there a few times, and on one of the passes a shadow appeared in back of the fly, and as I raised the rod the fish followed. I slowed the fly just a little, and Gabe and I both yelled as we watched the brown open his mouth to suck in the fly—another healthy twenty-one-incher. By this time we realized that we had been living so well that we had lost track of time and that we'd better get back to the boca and see what the royal party was up to.

We found the King ruling over a large amount of water and busy catching brookies from the local school with his guide, Angel. The King's brother was banished to a small cove nearby that didn't look very fishy. He'd waded out a few meters and was casting a whooly bugger in the same place with the exact same amount of line over and over. Gabe and I had ceased fishing and were sprawling about the vicinity when, to our surprise, grunting from the brother's direction announced that he was fast to a fish. The deep and even throbs of the rod indicated a heavy trout.

Gabe was the guide on duty, and went to assist him—as he seemed to be in a panic by the sound echoing out of that sheltered bay. The fish was pretty well subdued, but the huge man was doing what most overexcited neophytes do: he had reeled it in so far that the line was inside the rod. This is always dangerous, because the line to leader knot may catch on an eye and break the tippet if the fish takes flight. Gabe was trying to get him to wade back to shore so that we could beach the fish, as it was too big for the net. Reluctantly the fisherman waded toward shore and the five-pound brown was soon flopping about on the rocks.

Then a frantic scene started as the huge man pounced on the fish. He started pounding the big brown on a rock. But he was having some trouble killing it, because he wasn't hitting the fish's head on the rock—as is the common procedure—but was just bashing it without rhyme or reason, kicking the living shit out of the fish. His pullover hat covered one of his eyes and his cockeyed view through the thick glasses may have contributed to all the misdirected blows. Meanwhile, the count and the Russian woman had arrived to "help."

The count had a glass filled with his favorite mixture of coffee, wine, and whiskey. This was held in one hand while his ever-present pipe was in the other. He stumbled into the proceeding and quickly got line wrapped around his ankles in a sort of cat's cradle. He kept turning around to get untangled, but this made matters worse, contorting the rod alarmingly and dragging the reel clanking through the rocks. But this was just a sideshow to the main event, and soon the fish was sufficiently murdered and everyone got unraveled and tranquility returned to the primeval forest.

Gabe and I stood a few feet away from the brawl laughing like crazy. When it became obvious that the nobles had won the war, the big fellow turned toward us with a crazed look in his uncovered eye and asked how much longer we had to fish. Without waiting for a response, he asked if he could stay longer. He then got up and waded back to the same spot and commenced to cast in the exact same place for the next two hours. At the end of the day, when he waded back to shore, he asked Gabe if the fish lying there was his. After Gabe informed him that it was, he turned to me and said, "As if there is another five-pound brown lying there."

On the way back, everyone was in a joyous mood following the excellent fishing. While the royal family cavorted in the stern with their cocktails, the crew had coffee, pastry, and more than a few laughs in the cabin. I realized that I had never told the King about the big brookie. I started to go back and say something to him, but then thought better of it and watched the scenery slip by instead.

What's the big deal about catching a twenty-inch brookie anyway?

Chapter Fifteen

CRYING FOR THE ARGENTINE

■ ■ ■

I'm sitting in my favorite hotel room in Patagonia, killing time watching the news from Buenos Aires on the tele. It's 2002. All my clients have canceled their fishing trips due to the turmoil. I'm witnessing protests against the banks just now, and people are placing garbage against the doors. Some protesters are throwing eggs. A middle-aged man dressed in coat and tie dumps a load of horseshit on one bank's steps.

When the news reaches you guys in the States, it will have been elevated by the media into rioting and looting and the horseshit will be an "unknown brown substance suspected of being anthrax." Per usual only *Horse Fly* readers will have the real truth. In actuality these protesters are hardly desperados, and the scariest one I saw was an older woman with dyed red hair, wraparound mirror sunglasses, and the yellow teeth common to the BA tango set. (Another woman just held up a toilet seat with a picture of former President Carlos Menem pasted in the hole—cute.) There was some serious trouble last fall, and a number of Argentines were killed in real riots, but these troublemakers are the middle-class and rich Argentines—folks who have money and are pissed as hell that it's locked up. How you would you feel if they didn't let you at your own money?

Most people in the United States think of Argentina as an extension of Mexico; the farther south you go, the funkier things get. But Argentina is not a Third World country and has—or had—a large middle class that looks and lives much as we do in the States. They are of various European backgrounds and lead a similar lifestyle to Europeans or North Americans. They go on holiday, eat at fine restaurants, and generally live the good life. Just a few decades ago Argentina was one of the world's richest countries.

Gauchos at work

Of course there are plenty of poor folks who are busy being poor—like the poor all over the world. They're stuck and can't afford to "protest." The Argentines who can are leaving. I met a woman on the plane who was just returning from Quebec, where she is relocating her family. She and her husband are both research doctors who live in Buenos Aires. She is French and doesn't have ties to the Argentine like her husband does.

Family ties are so strong there that she knows there will be a lot of weeping and wailing when they move to Canada. But she said to me, "We have small children, and we are at the prime of our lives; we must do what's best for the kids. We can't wait ten years for things to change." Her kids are too young to understand what is happening, and when they were on the back porch of their BA apartment banging pots and pans in protest, her six-year-old said, "But mommy, we are not supposed to make noise." More dangerous rioters? She added another sad note: "I don't want to grow old in Argentina. It's no place for the old. The drug companies made deals with the government, and we can't even legally produce necessities like insulin. But we are anyway." It appears that

Geese, Rio Nuevo

there have been lots of deals. Carlos Menem sold the BA subways, the phone company, and the airline. The government has subsidized endless business enterprises, never to be paid back a centavo—except for money that went straight into the pockets of the politicians that arranged the loans.

Perhaps part of the Argentines' undoing is that they are just too damn nice and innocent for this vicious world—too trusting. A society of broke aristocrats who are "above money," as an American friend of mine living there put it. You see this in everyday dealings. For instance, it is not uncommon to buy something and find that, if the clerks don't have the right change, they will wave off a quarter, half peso, or even a dollar. Or they might ask you to stop by later—at your convenience—and pay then. They don't even use pennies, and just round everything off.

When I left New Mexico people said I was courageous to go to "riot-torn" Argentina. Buenos Aires is still one of the safest cites in the world, and the most dangerous part of my trip was probably my night at the Roach Way Inn in Albuquerque.

There are, of course, very few foreign tourists out here in the Andes this year and all is tranquil. The peso is now over two to the dollar. My room—con desayuno—

is $10 per night, a bife chorizo is about $5, and a cappuccino is a dollar. This Truchero finally finds himself a rich man for the moment. But thanks to real problems here— coupled with sensationalism inflicted by the press—I've no fishermen to guide. And like the Argentino, my fine taste is about to surpass my funds.

But I do have all this time on my hands and I hear the Trucheros are getting back together. . . . It's widely reported that they are drunk with trout fever and devaluation and gathering at an isolated river somewhere in outer Patagonia . . . Well, sign me up!

Claudio "Crazy Like Crazy" Campagna being preened by birdman Lorenzo Sympson.

CHAPTER SIXTEEN

ADRIFT IN PATAGONIA

■ ■ ■

At midmorning the Trucheros release four rafts into the lazy river. There are fifty miles of unspoiled, unfished water ahead and our guides assure us that few fishermen have ever floated this section of river. And floating is the only way to fish it, because it all lies within one huge estancia. Under Argentine law, all watercourses are public. But you have to get there without crossing private land, and the only access points are at either end of the giant ranch. It's a small river choked with brush, and we'll have to chop our way through in places. It's all a pretty big deal, and a lot of gear is required; we are weighted down with a chain saw, machetes, tents, tarps, and food for several days. All that weight will make hauling the rafts through the numerous shallows tough, too. But those problems lie around the bend, and for now all we envision are thousands of starving trout leaping at our flies.

In the first couple of miles la trucha have been under siege from walk-in fishermen and they are but small brookies and rainbows. As expected, the size of the fish increases as we drift farther away from the put-in, and the fishing turns really good whenever we enter stands of willows. If the angler can manage a cast under the branches, his chances of hooking a nice bow are very good. But the chances of hooking a limb are just a bit higher—about a foot above the water. Although we can't see the other boats through the brush, the tones of the other Trucheros' voices reveal whether they've hooked a fish or tree, and the sounds of cursing Trucheros, splashing trout, and ringing machetes is nonstop.

Being all old friends the Trucheros are a vocal lot of fishermen; our most hilarious member, marine biologist Claudio Campagna, is frantic catching, losing, and fighting fish. So pressed is he that he is forced to shorten the already brief phrase "ahi esta" (there it is) into "ayta." Claudio is an Argentine of Italian lineage who uses his hands to help him talk. But when he's fishing, his hands are employed holding the rod and can't flip and flop around to embellish his discourse—making him half mute. At one point the tragic loss of "the big" is just too much for his verbal expression and as mere words are insufficient to express the torment, he drops his rod, throws his hands to his head, and becomes "crazy like crazy."

Every fly fisherman should be fortunate enough to see how genuinely stupid a trout can be. And since an artificial fly has never tricked these fish—or their ancestors—they are ignorant of the proper protocol in the elite sport of fly-fishing. These silly creatures prefer dry flies submerged or dragged across the current, will grab a fly over and over again if not hooked on the first attempt, and then, most dumbfounding of all, will hold onto a fly and chew on it! We discover that when a "Chico" is trying to get caught we don't set the hook but instead wait for the little guy to expel the fly. But it can be a long wait.

I'm in heaven. I've fished many a wild river in my life, but never have I had so many miles of new water without the possibility of seeing another fisherman. And this is a gorgeous trout stream; riffles give way to pools that meander under bends and willows. These fish don't feed in the riffles as much as they do on other streams; they prefer slower water, but there is plenty of it in this flat land. In late afternoon, however, the river tightens and speeds up. We sail around a bend right into a wall of willows. The density of the brush stops us cold, and the fisherman in the bow starts clearing the brush with the machete. But he is not well versed in the use of the tool, and I hear a hiss when one of his strokes misses. My hasty first impression producing a pounding lump in my chest is that the raft has had a hole chopped in it. But I quickly realize that the hissing is man-made; it's our guide Ricardo's subtle way of suggesting that the bowman be careful. It's not an issue for long, anyway, because on the next swing he loosens the handle on the tool and the machete cartwheels off into ten feet of water. Fortunately there are two more of the long knives in the other boats, and we borrow one and chop our way out into the open.

Along toward dark—and ten miles downriver—we make camp under a tall stand of poplars. I quickly erect my little tent, suck down a yerba mate, and head to the river. There is a perfect place on the other side—and since I've only fished ten hours and a hundred trout, I start over to it. The biggest trout usually hang just downstream of brush, but these are difficult places to fish, and you must get the fly very close to the vegetation. There is fast water between me and the brush, and I wade out as far out as possible and try to reach over the current so the fly doesn't drag. The 14 Royal Wulff lands right behind the willow, and although I have my arm and rod extended as far as I can, the fly starts to drag just as a four-pound rainbow grabs for it. His big jaws shut behind the fly. Damn!

Since that's a big fish for this stream, I try changing to a nymph to see if he'll fall for that. But he's not interested, and I continue upstream. I'm soon consoled by the capture of about a half-dozen one-pounders. As I reel up and splash back to camp, the oval clouds over the Andes are fading from pink to gray in the day's final light. A flock of burrowing parrots, squawking incessantly, circle to roost in the poplars. These are big birds with greenish blue bodies and reddish brown chests; they fly in formation like waterfowl.

During our delicious asado someone suggests that the parrots will probably wake us up with their screeching before dawn. And since we are still eating at midnight (normal in Argentina), only our bird expert, Lorenzo Sympson, finds this prospect charming. He suggests that we all turn out early with him to see the parrots off. Lorenzo goes on to explain that this is a special microenvironment and birds that normally live much farther north and east are found here as well. His enthusiasm is infectious, and his knowledge of the natural world of Patagonia is so immense that even we myopic fly fishers are lured in. As the trip wears on and we grow bored with fish, we start noticing more and more birds and ask him about them.

Since Lorenzo now has the reader's interest, a word on him: although he does not have the status of Truchero he comes along on all these trips and has somehow become our spiritual leader because he is not a Truchero. But he helps us keep track of who has caught the biggest fish of the day and ribs the rest of us accordingly. He is not what you might think of when you picture a bird watcher. No thick glasses and nerdy bearing for this Anglo-Argentine of Scottish and English descent. He wears a sweat-stained hat and dusty clothes. He has traipsed endless miles of the Argentine—from the northern pampas to Tierra del Fuego. As a boy he spent his summers riding the range with the gauchos—leading quite the uncluttered life, he reports, for all they carried for food was salt and flour, and they'd simply kill a calf each night for dinner.

After one of his long jaunts, he returns with the unopened egg of a rhea, an ostrich-like bird. This is late in summer so it must be an egg that didn't hatch in spring. He tells us about finding these eggs when he was a kid growing up on the northern pampas. He and his kid sister would ride horseback across the great grasslands and collect the eggs to bring home for the kitchen. Of course being kids meant that they didn't think ahead and take a proper receptacle for storing the giant eggs. So Lorenzo would stick them down his sister's bombachos (baggy pants that fit tightly at the ankle). When the bombachos were full of eggs, they'd step the horse home—ever so lightly.

When the parrots start squawking at first light the next morning, I push the ear-plugs in deeper and go back to sleep, but hooves clacking on river rocks beside my tent awaken me a few minutes later. When I stick my head out of the tent, a couple of gauchos are trotting by with a huge long-legged lion dog trailing behind. The puesteros have come by to see who's about. They wave, exchange a few words with the guides, and go on their way.

But the fact that Argentine watercourses are public property galls the hell out of some landowners—and operators of some fly-fishing operations. And there can be confrontations. A friend of mine was hassled on one of Ted Turner's ranches, which he had legally accessed.

After café con leche in the morning, I head downriver on foot, long before the boats leave. I find some fish cruising and rising to mayflies in the shallows. The sight fishing has totally got my attention, but my concentration is interrupted when I hear "crazy like crazy" coming, and as they round the bend it seems as if one of us, or all of us at times, are hooked up with fish. I hop in the boat and find out that their best one is twenty inches; and now with perfect morning light behind us an even bigger fish takes my fly—several times actually, because just as it is about to eat, I get excited and pull the fly away. This guy is so hungry that he just spins in circles looking around for the fly, but each time he eats I jerk it out of its mouth. He acts more like a shark with the scent of blood in its nose than an intelligent trout. Finally, on about the fish's fourth assault, I wait until the big mouth actually closes on the fly, and the rainbow sails four feet out of the water when I set the hook. That insanely good fishing lasts for about an hour, and we settle back to the standard pace of about one decent trout every ten minutes or so. (Someone said at some point that "even the bad fishing is good.")

Hooked up in the holy land—Patagonia

About midway—some twenty-five miles downriver—a tragedy nearly occurs when the last machete sails off into about eight feet of water. But someone had wisely painted it red, and it is still visible. Claudio's son Leo is a skinny varmint, so everybody figures that he can slice through the water and reach the thing. But his dad gets "crazy like crazy" again and imagines that his son will be ensnarled by the sticks on the bottom of the river. So just as Leo is about to become the hero of the day, his dad hauls him out; one of the guides manages to get the thing after several dives.

But now that I have mentioned Leo, I had better explain him, too: he is the youngest member of the Trucheros and as such is known as Trucherito. He was inducted into the Trucheros in an elaborate ceremony that culminated with him being knighted by the gentle slap of a soft fly rod on the shoulder. Oddly, right as that was happening a priest friend of ours walked into the room, and when he witnessed our cultish behavior, wanted to exorcise the lot of us.

Leo's entry into the Trucheros came only after I had spent years on his fishing education, teaching him to cast and fish (plus, of course, he had to tie flies for the Trucheros). He was such a nice boy when I first met him, with the proper manners of an Argentine, but after spending so much time around us rude Yankees he can be a little brash. Unfortunately, I'm much to blame because I instructed him on Yankee mannerisms. At one point I stuck a toothpick in his mouth—something an Argentine would find uncouth to begin with—and then I had him slouch in his seat and repeat common American phrases out of the other side of his mouth, things like "get it yourself" and "I could care less." Unfortunately, the impressionable youth took my jesting seriously and hence, as his dad, Claudio, put it, he is now "a good son gone bad." Having created the monster, it is my karma to have this mangy polecat forever calling me viejo maricón.

After Argentine wine and beef, the Trucheros are in fine form and the stories abound. Nothing upsets a true Truchero more than the loss of "the big." And we are all intrigued by the story of Claudio's missing a thirty-inch fish the previous season. The story isn't so much about the fish itself but about the reaction the excitable Truchero had, and guide Marcos says that the wailing, wringing of hands, and rolling of eyes filled all Patagonia. It was even suggested that a poem be composed about the event—something perhaps to equal the epic *The Gaucho Martín Fierro* by José Hernández—The Truchero Claudio Campagna.

I get a good sleep after that chuckle and wake up early in the morning to do some downriver exploring with Lorenzo. We leave early and get well ahead of the boats before "crazy like crazy" alarms all the birds.

And by now I have caught so many fish that I've turned into a birder, and birds are everywhere on this misty pink morning. Lorenzo gets all atwitter when he sees a black swallow, a bird he never expected to see so far from the Atlantic coast. But we are descending toward that ocean—and the vegetation is thinning and the hills are leveling out as we pull away from the Andes. Wigeon sail by with their peeping call that sounds like the call of our North American variety—"not a proper duck call,"

Lorenzo says. A hidden critter soon makes a raucous call—so loud that we investigate, as Lorenzo thinks it might be a guanaco; but it turns out to be a brown pintail. Mourning doves crisscross the river at dazzling speeds, and the introduced Gambel's quail make their peacocklike call off in the brush. Later, after the sun has created thermals, we get a special treat as we see two condors uncharacteristically close to the river.

By the time the crew reaches us, I am ready to go back to fishing, and I hop in the boat just as the fish start feeding on inchworms. Los Trucheros are always looking for some new challenge to make the game just a little more interesting, and whenever we see a rise back under the trees—where the inchworms live—we try to drive a tight cast into there. The fly has to be literally bounced in, and we try to make such a tight loop that the fly hits well short of the target and then skips across the surface, to land, we hope, way back under the low-slung willows. If we throw successfully we are usually treated to the sight of a fine rainbow eating. Although many a tree is hooked, it is some of the best dry fly-fishing I have ever had. I change places with Marcos, the guide and oarsman, so that he can get into some of the action too. Before long he is whooping and hollering like Claudio. Once it is discovered that I can row the boat, I take over for the other guides too. That's OK, because half the fun for me is seeing a fellow fishing guide have a good time.

Nick Streit with seaside accomplice

PART IV

SALT WATER

Chapter Seventeen

MAN'S SUPERIORITY TO FISH

■ ■ ■

Several years ago I spent the winter in a bright yellow house on a remote Bahamian island. It had four rooms, a table with three and one-half chairs, a bed with both top and bottom sheets, a sofa kinda thing, a hot plate, and a gas fridge. What more could you want for $200 a month? The front of the house even had a couple of bougainvilleas, a scrawny mango tree, and greenish fuzz that looked somewhat like a lawn.

But the backyard was the ocean itself! When the wind and tide were up, waves would beat against the coral shore and drench the house in spray. The view out to sea was a typical Bahamian one: pastel shades of green and blue stood against a white sand bottom, and the few coral heads appeared almost black, darker than the more extensive grass patches. (A novice boatman will zigzag around all these dark bottoms until he learns to tell the dangerous coral from the harmless grass.) Just to the south, the strong currents of a large saltwater river drained and filled the beautiful bay.

It all blended together to make a pretty fishy environment, so snorkel gear and spear were kept ready at the back door. I had several thousand miserable trout flies to tie, and I needed quality breaks from the boredom. So when conditions were suitable—when tide, sun, and appetite were in sync—I would grab the Hawaiian sling and proceed to the Caribbean to try and stab some lunch. I would manage to impale something now and then, but as often as not I would swim to the back door empty-handed.

But you gotta have nutritious fish if you live on South Andros Island. The one little store had only a sampling of fruit, some canned food, frozen meat, and Little Debbie treats—all brought by mail boat at very high prices. (The Little Debbies cost three times the price marked on the box.) This sparse diet was supplemented by ingestion of a popular drink called Vitamalt. If you have just arrived from the bountiful States, the foul, vitamin-laden concoction is nearly impossible to swallow. But after a few months of coconuts, canned spaghetti, and Little Debbies, your malnourished body will only holler MORE when the gummy, brown brew touches the lips—and you'll drain the bottle in two or three good pulls.

When you reach the point where you crave Vitamalt, it's time to step up the seafood intake. The fishies had been outsmarting me pretty bad, in part due to my shortcomings with the spear, but as I'm handy with rod and reel, it wasn't long before my son, Nick, and I had developed a new style of fishing that put the hurtin' on those poor fish.

They were too spread out for us to be able to catch them consistently by randomly casting here and there. As all fishermen know, there are always more fish "there" than "here," and the chances of your fly landing near some delicious fellow . . . well, that is where the four-letter word "luck" enters into the equation. On the other hand, if you know the exact whereabouts of said underwater lunch, that takes luck right out of the picture.

The operation went something like this: Nick snorkeled over likely territory while I awaited instructions from shore, ten-weight fly rod in hand. We found that if Nick raised his head out of the water and yelled to me, the fish would often be gone by the time he got his head back under. Consequently, we came up with an elaborate set of hand signals so that Nick could relate to me what he was seeing without having to stick his head above water, remove his mask, and holler.

The first signal started simply with one finger raised out of the water and aimed toward the quarry. The vigor of the motion indicated the edibility of the critter. For instance, the flat-tasting French grunt would get far less finger-stabbing enthusiasm than a delicious grouper found hiding in its den.

As I waded toward the targeted fish, Nick would give me additional hand signals. A wiggling hand meant that the fish was swimming off. If the creature appeared to be just moseying along, the hand would also swim along casually. But, if the fish were heading

Sign near Congo Town airport, Andros Island, Bahamas

for "there," the hand would wiggle powerfully in that direction. As I got closer, other signals would come into play. A wading angler bothers a fish more than a swimming one, so if the fish showed signs of nervousness, a halting sign would be given—a raised palm meant STOP. When the fish settled down, the index finger wiggled the universal "come here" signal. When in casting range, I would get more precise instructions about what the fish was up to. If it was feeding, the fingers would be extended and mimic a mouth opening and closing.

Finally, it was time for the cast—and time to show those finny varmints who was boss. Fish in shallow water are spooky, and it's always important not to brain them with the fly. So Nick would direct me to cast somewhat away from the fish. We discovered that with some species it was preferable to fish with a slack line, and such a fish would just sit in front of the fly and tread water as it studied the proposed meal. The animal's indecision would be portrayed by a horizontal wobbling hand—maybe yes, maybe no. With the line slack like that, the spotter would have to inform the angler when to set the hook. With our system, if the fish took the fly, the snorkeler would signal strike by raising a clenched fist—another sign of man's superiority over fish, Vitamalt, and blind luck!

Wilderness bonefish

CHAPTER EIGHTEEN

BLUE HOLE SNAPPER

■ ■ ■

I worked several winters in the bonefishing business on South Andros Island, Bahamas. The island is one hundred miles long and inhabited only on its eastern shore—where channels have been blasted through the coral so large boats can land. The area is not frequented by the island-hopping sailboats that visit other Caribbean islands because of its shallow nature. (It also lacks the kind of charm and sophistication that would entice the Margaritaville set.) South Andros has a distant, voodoo feel that is appropriate for a gateway to vast amounts of truly wild wetlands: the interior, southern, and western sides of the island have miles of saltwater creeks, lakes, and blue holes, holding endless supplies of fish.

Although fishing operators on South Andros can and do occasionally travel into these remote places, they can't really fish the farthest or shallowest waters on a daily basis. And travel into such areas is limited to the brightest hours of the day (8 a.m. to 4 p.m.), when visibility into the water is good. Without good light it's all too easy to run aground or ruin a prop; then the boatman is faced with making twenty miles back across land, sea, and swamp to the town of Mars Bay. These constraints make for short fishing days and eliminate the most exciting times of the day—early and late, when bonefish are hungry and tailing.

The run there must also be made out in the open, across exposed ocean where coral heads and waves must be dealt with. If the sea is up, the little flats boats must be babied through the waves. If there is only a breeze, you are bounced over the smaller waves for so long that all your teeth will be loose by the time you reach your destination. This outside ocean run is more comfortable and safer in larger V hull boats; but once you arrive, you won't have access to the shallowest water.

Another way to fish these waters is to maneuver a yacht close by and fish from a flats boat you've towed along for that purpose. The inherent dilemma with this is that it can be problematic and time consuming to acquire the yacht. You must move to the city, go to college, get a high-paying job, and work so hard that you have a heart attack—after which you reevaluate your life, finally buying the yacht—and only then, at long last, go fishing. But this schedule hasn't allowed you any time to learn to fish; consequently, by the time you are good at it, you're dead.

A superior plan that better suits the financially challenged angler is to get a tent, a fish grill, and some canned food, then throw them in a little boat and head out. And being in the financial bracket of camper rather than yachtsman means that your time is not all that valuable, so you can spend considerably longer periods out among the fish.

My "yacht" was the tiny Diki boat, and although too small for clients, it was fantastic for one person. Since the foam-filled little vessel drew less than five inches of water, it was feasible to explore some areas that couldn't be reached with other boats.

Equipped with plenty of fuel, food, water, and a plastic coated map, I took off over a gentle sea to explore and fish. One of my main missions was to bring back scrumptious snapper filets for guests at the bonefish lodge. I'm all for catch-and-release, but when the occasion arises to catch, kill, and eat, I get downright serious. The other goal of the excursion was one that I also warmed to—finding the best fishing for clients.

Heading out alone into such a wilderness of water is a powerful, scary experience for a landlubber. The safety net is the seriousness of the business itself. Because when you consider the things that can go wrong out there—your motor can quit, you can get sick, or cut, or tip over, get shark bit, sting ray stung, hijacked by drug smugglers, or hit by a meteorite, you tend to be up on your toes. But what the hell, we only go around once. . . . right?

I traveled south at three-quarter throttle for about an hour and a half and then started looking for the entrance of the first creek that I planned to explore. The map showed that it had a narrow entrance, and it took some poking around the mangroves before I found it. It was protected from the ocean's waves and I could study the bottom even though it was thirty feet down. It was reminiscent of being out in the open ocean on one of those rare dead-calm days when you can see a very long way in the clear water. I gazed into a world of coral, sand, and waving sea plants. On the white sand bottom a small sea turtle lay motionless, and a few feet off from it a giant crayfish crawled the ocean floor—all good signs, because those creatures wouldn't be there if the place was frequented that much.

I continued up the narrow channel, the tide ebbing and the current ripping out of the creek. It created a big whirlpool in one spot where there were thousands of pilchards. Silver clouds of the choice bait flashed in the morning light. I grabbed my rod, threw a big popper in the deep hole, and slashed it across the surface a few times. Nothing happened, so I moved up the creek. The map didn't indicate much for flats up there, but it was an interesting place and I continued upstream, winding through a maze of brush-covered islands. This is what gray snapper love—fairly deep water and brush—but there was no sign of them.

Then the creek spread out over a marled bottom and a couple of bonefish tails flashed up ahead. They were rooting around some mangrove plants, and I turned the motor off and poled toward them. When almost in range, I gave one strong push on the pole and then, as I slid quietly toward the fish, I laid the pole down as gently as possible. Once I got the rod up, I sent the fly as close to the fish as I dared, then let it sit and wait until one of those tailing bones moseyed toward the fly. And then one was right over the fly, and I started the retrieve. He saw it and his tail went down as he made a quick motion forward. The tail rose above the surface as he picked up the fly. After I applied the strip strike, he zinged off through the mangrove. The line almost instantly got wrapped around a bush and broke, but I knew that I wouldn't catch him in all that mess anyway. I got to see the best part—the take. Whether it's a fifteen-pound peacock bass exploding after a foot-long fly, a trout slurping a dry, or a barracuda creaming a popper, I'm addicted to that take.

I decided to try to see the whole creek, so I poled through the tiny flat and found some deepish calm water beyond. And there was the wily gray snapper at last—a whole crowd of them in a still pool between the bushes. I dropped a Clouser minnow in among them and one grabbed it before it sank a foot. It was a nice one of about two pounds that pulled like mad, and I put another cast in there, but in typical gray snapper fashion, the smart fish ignored it—having learned in just one lesson that eating a fly will precipitate their extraction from the pool. But I cast into a different hole and caught another—then cast to another hole for another fish, and then when I ran out of new spots to fish it was time for the real fishin'—and time to find some bait.

So I put on a wire leader and a somewhat larger fly, and started casting and stripping here and there, and before long a small 'cuda was on the line. Barracuda (or barrie, as the Bahamians call it) is a very good fish to eat, and snapper concur with that assessment. A hunk of flesh was quickly put on a hook and lofted into the snapper hole. I could see these fish perfectly in the still pool and it was just a riot watching the poor things trying to resist eating the meat. Of course that first cast was gobbled almost instantly, but from then on they grew shyer and shyer until, after I caught two or three, they left it alone.

These were backwoods snapper and not hip to the routine, and the next and final phase was rough on them. It was time to chum, so scales, pieces of gut, flesh, and fins went flying into the hole. As the meat dispersed slowly downward in a milky cloud, first one then another fish started to eat. My hook was hidden in one of the hunks, and a few more fish entered the boat. Finally, with no more meat or cards up my sleeve it was time to leave the somewhat smaller, but better educated, school of fish.

So it was back out to the sea and down the coastline, next stop on the map being Eagle's Nest Creek. Its entrance was easier to find as it contained considerably more water than the last creek. I went up it a bit and found it kind of spooky—the shoreline was desolate, bare coral with little vegetation, and the creek itself would have been dangerous to run looking into the afternoon sun, as it had a strong current and went from deep to shallow instantly in many places. And since I couldn't find anywhere to camp, I turned around and headed back to the coast to find some higher sand to sleep on. There would be more of a breeze out there by the sea, which would help to keep the skeeters away. I found a spot within a half mile of the mouth, and after grilled snapper, some sleep, and morning coffee, I was ready for a new adventure.

It was an easy run up the river in the morning with the light behind me, and there was no problem avoiding the shallows. Coming to a big bay, I wrapped the bow rope around my waist and started wading. I saw a push up ahead, but the fish were going away. I slowly made my way over to the shore and, after securing the boat, ran up ahead of them and, once in position, cast in front of the little school. There were a couple of nice fish in the bunch and one of the better ones took the fly. I landed this very nice bone of about six pounds and split because the bottom there was not pleasant to wade, being soft and lumpy. With all the miles of flats on South Andros, there was no need to kill myself walking over yucky bottom.

I caught that fish and hundreds of others on a fly my son and I invented when he was twelve. The shit fly has an ugly name (this is the salty shit fly, not to be confused with the shit fly nymph for trout), but it is an accurate description, as it is made of brown mottled chenille with bead chain eyes and brown feathers out the back. As we learned more and more about bonefish—and bone fishermen—we realized that if a bonefish is hungry and your fly has the right weight for the situation, it will eat almost anything. Matching the color of the bottom you're fishing with the fly itself helps, but it's not that important when fishing remote water. Most fly fishermen love to make a big deal out of exact shades, exact number of wraps of each material, an exacting angle for the feathers—too damn exacting! When one such fly technician saw some of my clumsy jobs, he said, "Taylor ties shit flies"—so we went him one step better and created an official shit fly.

On days that were not fishy I tied trout flies commercially; but once or twice a week the weather would get nice, and I would even keep my son, Nick, out of school if it looked like he could learn more in the salt air than in the Bahamian school system. If we needed flies for the day, one of us tied them as the other made breakfast and lunch for the trip. After I'd been cooped up tying all week, complicated flies were not on the menu!

Back on Eagle's Nest Creek, I continued up the river of salt water to another big lake, but I didn't like the looks of it either. Too deep for bones, and a lousy bottom to boot; maybe this place was just not going to work out. But, after looking at the map, there seemed to be extensive flats farther back. The small-scale map seemed to show a tiny passage going in and I was in the Diki boat, which could float on spit. I found the opening and started to pole up it. Fortunately I was riding in with a spring tide, but the tiny creek was still more like a parched New Mexico trout stream than a piece of ocean, and I had to get out and haul the boat over some of the lower spots. I wondered if anyone else had ever gotten a boat back in there, and then realized that I would have to come out at the same time the next day so that I could make the same tide.

As I was riding the flooding current in, who should be riding out against it, heading upstream as it were, but a gang of bones. I waited for them to work into range. It was like sight fishing for trout in the current, and I was mending line and drifting the fly in front of the fish. It was obvious that I was "back there" by the attitude of these animals as they swam right next to me without spooking. I caught them all the way down into the lake.

By the mouth of the creek there was an egret's nest about three feet off the water. When I walked up the mom flew off a few feet, but the fuzzy white babies just looked at me kinda dopey.

When I got to the lake there were bonefish tailing near the creek mouth. And beyond them, out in the lake, water was being pushed this way and that by three or four different schools! The flat was an easy one to wade, too, shallow and firm. The bottom was dark, which made spotting fish tough, but those dark flats seemed to be popular with the bones. I introduced the shit fly into the lake and it was well received. I caught a nice mess of bonefish in the area, but I needed to do some exploring, so I headed off to the north.

I was, of course, checking out the flats, but I also wanted to see if it might be possible to find a passage from this creek into Windy Creek. The part of Windy that is adjacent is crammed full of bonefish, and finding a connecting channel would cut lots of time and miles off getting to this hidden lagoon. As I moved toward Windy Creek, the dark bottom gave way to a light one and consequently the number of fish thinned out. But when you did see one over such a light bottom it was way fun, because you got lots of foreplay and had plenty of time to intercept them.

"Nervous water"—surrounding a huge school of bonefish

I did see a BIG fish from a ways off, coming straight at me, and I had a perfect opportunity. The fly landed several feet in front of him and when it looked like he was close I started the retrieve. He found something amiss and sped off in the other direction. I was continually amazed at how smart large bonefish were—even when they had probably never been bothered by fishermen before.

I headed farther and farther inland looking for the passage to Windy and finally saw a channel of water that belonged to that creek, separated from the water I was standing in by only twenty feet. I looked around for a solution but there was no getting around, or over, those few feet of land. It would have been no sweat with a sea kayak—just carry it across—but even the lightweight Diki boat was too heavy here.

I went back to the mouth of the creek. From there the lake also ran off in another direction. I was hoping to find somewhere to camp, but I hadn't seen anyplace more than a foot above sea level all day and soggy camping sucks. I was able to motor down to that end of the lake because it was several feet deep. It led up onto a flat, and when I cut the motor and stood I saw three unusual things. The first and closest was a small, perfectly round blue hole in the flat. (A blue hole, for those who don't know, is an underwater cave that goes straight down into the earth.) I slid by it quietly and observed many fish. This brought me closer to the next unusual sight, dry white sand shining on the bank. And just beyond the sand lay the third little oddity, a great mound with an osprey sailing over it.

I checked out the nest before making camp; it was made of sticks and was three or four feet in diameter, with its summit just above eye level. There must have been chicks or eggs inside, because mom and dad were screaming and diving at me. One would hover a few feet above, while the other circled and threatened with its talons. When I felt confident that they were not going to scalp me, I peered over the top of the nest and was suddenly eyeball to eyeball with two half-grown chicks. I wondered if this could be the eagle's nest that the creek was named after. But the creek was probably named years and years ago. Could the nest have been there that long? (Several years later, an ornithologist friend told me that the nest has probably been in use for a very long time.)

While making camp I shifted my attention to plotting a strategy for fishing the blue hole. It could be an unplundered goldmine of big gray snapper. I came up with a plan that required meat, and I set out from camp looking for a bonefish to use as bait. It didn't take long to slay one, and I went back to camp and cut it into bite-size pieces. Then, poling the boat, I quietly approached the blue hole. The breeze and sun were perfect, both at my back. I dropped anchor and my little yacht swung around and the rope pulled tight just on the edge of the blue hole, putting me into position looking almost straight down into the unknown depths of the thirty-foot-diameter abyss. It had a mysterious quality about it, because there wasn't a clue as to where, how far, or how deep it went. I could see some small and medium-sized snapper on the edges, but what other fish lived down there? In another blue hole, we had found a school of tarpon. There was only one way to find out what lurked in the depths . . .

I got ready for fast action: put the bait and chum on the deck, and placed pliers, knife, and towel handy. The sun was almost down, and according to the rules of nature, these creatures should have been getting hungry. I followed the same routine as I did with the other snappers the day before, and threw the Clouser in there. About fifty one-pounders to two-pounders pounced on the fly. This was gonna be rich! Several landed flopping at my feet before they got wise. Step two: bait change to a single large hook and hunks of bonefish. This brought some larger fish into the boat, maybe two and a half pounds. Eventually (you know the drill) the catching stopped. But by that time there were a couple of hundred nice snapper hanging around the edge of the blue hole. They looked poised and waitin' for something to happen—so, step three: chum, free food, come and get it. They went berserk. The surface erupted; a slashing, churning, feeding frenzy ensued. I was hauling them out of there as fast as I could, but they were fighting harder and harder as the size of the fish got bigger and bigger. Rebaiting is a pain, so I decided to put on some fifty-pound test and a large white fly.

When I had that accomplished and looked back in the hole my mouth dropped, because the crowd of two- and three-pounders had been replaced by some very large snapper. There were no fewer than a hundred of them—all over four pounds!—on the edges of the hole. And from the blue depths a very large barracuda had emerged and planted itself right in the middle of the proceedings. I knew his intentions were in conflict with mine, so I hooked bonefish tail onto the fly and smacked it on his head. After an instantaneous take he went racing across the flat with it at about a hundred miles an hour. We struggled for a while before he bit through the fifty-pound tippet, but—mission accomplished—he was gone.

I threw some chum along with another big white fly in there and started fighting those huge snapper. This was a great opportunity to fill the freezer and I wanted those big, tasty fillets in the boat. But they fought so hard, the ten-weight Sage was bent over into my gut and I had so much pressure on that when I got one to the surface it popped out of there as if it had been shot from a cannon, landing in the boat with a bounce. It was like the commercial fishermen who haul those giant tuna into the boat. Absolutely wild fishing.

I spent half the next morning filleting fish. The ice in the cooler was gone, so I had to hurry home. The ride back was not like the easy one I had coming down. I had the tide all wrong, so I had to return out in the sea. At one point I was forced to go around an island and had to crawl over huge waves—scary business for a landlubber in a tiny Diki boat.

From left to right: marlin, author, dorado

CHAPTER NINETEEN

MARLIN

■ ■ ■

Every few years I get to fish with my pal Keith Loveless in some exotic spot. Not that many times, but enough that I've had a good overview of what he's up to out in the blue. My first trip with him was off the Yucatán coast in Mexico. He had towed his boat there from the States. Hauling a boat overland across Mexico is just asking for trouble, and he got plenty of it. He describes one stimulating event like this:

> The boat trailer started fishtailing, so we stopped and saw the boat was sliding off the back. It was too heavy to pick up and reposition, and there was no water to float it on and put it back that way. So there was nothing to do but go forward real fast and slam on the brakes and hope that it would shift the boat back where it belonged. But that worked a little too well, and the boat ended up poked into the camper. So I popped the clutch trying to send it backward a little and broke the drive shaft and the springs on the truck. Mind you, I was a hundred miles from anywhere in the Yucatán jungle, and so I crept to the next town on the front axle of the four-by-four. I then called Lorelei to bring the broken hardware down by plane.

Here it should be mentioned that Keith is blessed with a wonderful wife who fetches him such stuff with a smile.... Well, it's more like half a smile that rises up toward an eyebrow raised in the form of a question mark.

Along with equipment problems, physical catastrophes seem to punctuate his life. I'm searching for the right word here, because I wouldn't describe him as being accident-prone. He once told me, "Well, you gotta be out there doing stuff." He broke both of his legs at once in a construction accident—an injury from which he still suffers. He has impaled himself on so many big hooks and gaffs that he now wears hiking shoes in his boat.

But he plants a lot of those sharp points in fish too. It's been a long trip over the learning curve for him across many a fishless nautical mile. His lust for the billed fishes of the sea started in the Florida Keys and then moved to the Baja of Mexico. But it wasn't until Keith found his way to Kona, Hawaii, that he got into big marlin. Kona is on the western side of the Big Island of Hawaii. The winds blast the opposing side of the island, causing a big eddy to form on the lee shore, right in front of Kona, putting the fishing very close at hand. To give you an idea how close, the previous season Keith hooked a 600-pound blue marlin while he was fishing solo. He had caught a 400-pounder two days before while alone, so he knew what he was in for. When he saw what kind of fish he was latched onto, he used his free hand to grab the cell phone and call up a friend who was in his house in Kona. The guy drove down to the dock, got in his boat, and went out and helped Keith land the huge marlin.

Both he and his son Tyler have gotten very proficient at catching fish there. As my son, Nick, and I got to the dock, I heard a charter captain say to Keith, "You've only been here a couple of days and you are already showing us up." This sounded like promising news, and we knew we were on the right track when Keith nicknamed our father/son group the "murder squad." Nick and I have only slight experience in this form of angling, but when afield we do tend to put up the meat. It's true that luck plays a big part in trolling the vast Pacific, but some boats are a lot luckier than others, and the "granders" (1,000-pound marlin) that Keith is looking for are caught by the same boats over and over. Murder squads no doubt man these lucky boats, so when luck strikes, murderous instincts guide the instantaneous decisions and responses that arise during such a battle. Things come down too quickly for the hesitant, and hesitation brings bad luck, and bad luck can be serious in this game—for unlike the tiny trout I'm used to, these beasts can actually hurt you. Fishermen have been stabbed by leaping bills—and dragged, flung, and flipped overboard.

My touch of seasickness left me as soon as we hooked an ono. The small wahoo could barely struggle against the hundred-pound line and telephone-pole rod. I mentioned to Keith that it would be a nice fish on the fly rod, and he said that we were really fishing for marlin. These little ono were just "bonus" fish. We came up with a second one pretty quickly.

I have always thought this type of fishing was boring and mindless, but I started seeing that this wide ocean could be read like any other water. We always had someone in the crow's nest looking for debris, birds, and currents. Debris would most likely be in the current lines that reveal themselves as slicks across the surface. They are easy to spot if you are up in the Kona hills looking downward, but it takes lots of scanning through Polaroid sunglasses to detect them right at sea level. They often appear as a different shade from the rest of the drink.

Keith told us these currents vary in nature and carry different types of debris. What we were looking for was a current with plenty of larger junk, because that's where the larger fish linger. Tyler was in the crow's nest and headed us toward "a bunch of shit in the water." He sounded pretty excited, and an instant later, bam—fish on! It was Nick's turn to land this mahi, and we went back around, made another pass by the debris, and caught the mate.

We approached a buoy that was out several miles. These buoys are placed to attract fish, and by the looks of all the boats around this one, there was a fish-catchin' party going on. Fish could be seen breaking, and without a word of communication Keith and Tyler were instantly busy pulling lines and rerigging them. Nick and I had no idea of what they were doing, but they smelled big fish and within a few minutes the desired quarry was flopping about the boat—in the form of a small tuna.

Keith motioned me over to show me how he rigs this big bait using needle, thread, and a big circle hook. He then tossed it overboard and let out about a hundred feet of line, and then attached the line to a cleat with a rubber band. From the rubber band toward the rod he freed up another fifty feet or so of line and dumped that out of the boat. That way—as he described to us—when a fish takes, the rubber band snaps and alerts us to impending action. While the boat and crew prepare for the fight, the fish will have a chance to eat the bait on the fifty feet of slack line. During that brief period, the boat is powered up, and when the line pulls tight it will be time to set the big hook.

He was just polishing off the dissertation when the rubber band snapped. Seems there was a fish large enough to eat a three-pound bait sitting right under the boat! This didn't surprise me because the captain had just told us what would happen—but it sure shocked the shit out of our skipper, and Keith's murderous instincts froze for a second. Then it was all action; Tyler fit me with the fighting belt and directed me to the chair in the bow. Then I was handed the rod and commanded to "reel like hell." But when I came up tight to the fish it strongly resisted the arrangement, and line screamed off the reel. When the fish finally stopped that initial run, I tried to reel; but it was nearly impossible to turn the handle, and it wasn't long before I had to stop and rest.

We of course hoped that we had a marlin on, but we didn't know. I had never been connected to a fish of this magnitude and consequently had no position to speculate from, but I got a sinking feeling when Keith mentioned the word "shark." I have hooked a number of them and know what the fight of one feels like—and this felt like that. And then we saw the line coming toward the surface, but there was so much line out that we didn't know where the fish actually was. We were looking all over the horizon for the jump.

And then, way the hell out there—behind many tossing waves—a silver marlin leapt from the sea. We yelled our salutes with each jump. But he didn't stay up for long, and when he sounded, we went back to the dogged deepwater fight. We didn't have a real fighting chair on board, and I was used to fighting a fish with my scrawny old arms and didn't know how to use my whole body. So I was fading fast but getting words of encouragement from everybody—except skipper Keith, who said, "Just reel the God damn thing in, will ya." (He speculated that it was "only" 200 pounds.)

I was so uncomfortable in the chair that we decided to get me over on the side of the boat and see how I would do standing. The belt was too loose and kept slipping, and the butt of the rod was wildly searching for footing over my family jewels. My back started to cramp and I felt bad. But not as bad as the marlin, because then, all of a sudden, an odd shake ran up the line, and right after that the fish started to come in. But when it got straight under the boat it started taking line straight down—and I couldn't do a thing to stop it. I was pulling as hard as I could and was by now physically very uncomfortable, but the line kept going out of the reel. About that time,

Keith said that it might be dead and sinking. Tyler got his shoulder under the rod to slow the descent. I told Keith that after that odd wiggle there hadn't been any sign of life, just a lot of what felt like dead weight, and that maybe the wiggle had been the animal's death throes.

By then I was starting to get faint and fumbly. My back was almost stove up and I decided to give it up and called for that he-man son of mine to come and relieve me. He's all shoulders, but when he got the rod in his hands he couldn't get a turn on the reel either. Nick tried to pump it up but the sweat built on his red face. I was relieved to see that it wasn't just me. We were now pretty sure that the fish was dead and that it had probably been tail-wrapped all along. (Hence the sluggo fight that reminded me of shark.) Pulling it backward had forced water into its gills and drowned the poor fish—which was a shame, because we would have released it. The only way to bring in such dead weight is by hand—lining it in inch by inch. Tyler put on leather gloves and started to hand-over-hand the line up, and Nick hauled back on the rod at the same time. But there were at least 400 feet of line out, and this was going to be a long process.

I had an opportunity to recuperate and was just starting to settle into the wonderful feeling of not being attached to that fish when Nick yelled, " Mahimahi." I was spellbound by the sight of this brilliant animal, and then somebody else said, "Get the fly rod." It was stowed under me, and I had to dig through some gear to get it—a fly was attached, but it still needed to be assembled. Keith started feeding the fish and I glanced over and saw the animal race by and grab some of the meat. Keith said, "He'll stick around now." I finally had the rod together and cast my foot-long fly to the hot fish that wasn't ten feet from the boat. A couple of strips and he busted the fly, but we didn't connect. This was one of the most awesome sights I had ever seen in nature: indescribable shades of blue, green, and yellow on fire as the predator hunted for the meal it had just lost. I dropped the fly in front of it again and somebody yelled, "Pull it fast." I made a long sweep of the fly rod and the fish almost bumped its head on the bow of the boat as it engulfed the fly.

We all gave this fish a cheer too—as it scrambled away from the boat in a series of emerald leaps. Keith suggested that I let it stay out a ways so that it didn't get tangled with the marlin line. So I eased off and let the fish swim around in the distance.

Meanwhile, our boys had continued to make progress on the marlin. They couldn't stop taking line, because when pulling in a heavy fish or other object that is not coming the easy way (in this case, headfirst), it is important that the momentum never stops, and that the object doesn't get a chance to start falling again. Soon they reached the rubber band, meaning that there were a hundred feet of line left.

The mahimahi had tired of the waiting game and, rejuvenated after swimming around on a near slack line, it started to dive straight down and I realized that we had better get it in the boat before it fouled the number one line. So I started pumping it up on the thirteen weight. Keith didn't want the mahi in the boat before the marlin, because they go ballistic when landed and are hard to kill. But we didn't have much choice, and we set the gaff in fish number two. When we got it in the boat, Keith whacked it with the bat and all hell broke loose. The fish flopped, shimmied, and shook so violently that it sprayed blood and slime throughout the stern.

At this inopportune moment, the marlin came into view. The boys informed us that it was not tail-wrapped but hooked near the anus. Keith tossed the mahi in the fish bag as the marlin reached the boat. Tyler got a grip on the bill, and Keith grabbed the gill plate, and they started hauling it over the gunwale. Tyler was soon on his back with his feet pressed against the inside of the boat for leverage, but he was sliding in mahi juice. With a giant effort, they hauled a little over half of the immense fish into the boat, and with Nick pushing from the other end, they persuaded the lighter half to come in the rest of the way.

Lots of howls and backslapping followed, and we then snapped photos of me with the two fish. It was a lot to fit in the frame: rods and reels and duo of fish—one of them over ten feet long—and author with swelled head. And we tried to include the incredible sight of a snow-capped volcano in the background.

Although it was still early, that about made a day's fishing, and the "murder squad" headed in. We were all surprised when the beast was hoisted up and weighted in at 361 pounds. Not a huge marlin by Kona standards, but by far the biggest fish of this angler's life.

Author's Note: I would like to inform any readers who are trying to keep up with Captain Keith that I just ran into him and he told me that he had been "doing stuff":

he had just come from the Pacific Northwest, where he hooked a thirty-five-pound salmon on Zebco rod and reel that straightened out his hook. He then—in the same locale—tried to save the life of a member of one of the area's endangered species and, failing to accomplish the rescue, ate the animal for dinner. He had caused—and cleaned up—a toxic spill on an island in the Pacific Ocean. And he was on his way to collect (by bullet) a four-year-old bison from a nearby Indian reservation.

Nightfall approaches the lonely mountain.

PART V

HUNTING

Chapter Twenty

LIFE AND DEATH ON THE SIERRA ALTO

■ ■ ■

It was the first day of deer season, but I was cooped up in the car waiting for the weather to break. It really wasn't so bad stretched out in the back of my SUV, munching trail mix, snoozing now and then, and reading. I had scouted the area the day before under clear skies and had seen lots of deer, antelope, and turkey, a herd of nine bull elk, one overly large bear—and not one human soul.

But that was yesterday, and those long blue vistas were now short gray ones as rain-soaked clouds swept this lonely volcanic mountain. At about three o'clock the wind relaxed, the rain eased to an occasional plinking on the roof, and the sun added a few weak rays of hope. I figured that every drenched critter in the animal kingdom would soon be up and about, and I hastily grabbed my backpack and started up the mountain.

I stumbled onto two bull elk in the first canyon I crossed. They galloped down the yellow slope and ran above a herd of antelope that were grazing on the fringe of the mountain. Cows appeared as blotches in the distance beyond those animals. I imagined—just for an instant—that all those cows out in the grasslands were buffalo. Oh, well . . . what a bountiful world it must have been—way back when.

But it's still pretty rich, and when I turned my binoculars uphill, there were two herds of deer in small meadows above me. Not being able to put horns on any of them from this distance, I planned a route that would take me close to both groups. The first bunch turned out to be all does and fawns, so I continued up. Upon getting to where I thought the others would be, I slipped behind a tree and started glassing the area through the branches. As often happens, while I was looking for them in the distance, the herd suddenly appeared much closer, in a little basin just below me. There was a buck among the does. I lay down, used my pack for a rest, and shot him when he turned sideways. He leapt up in the air at the shot—a heart shot—but I fired again to be sure, and he went down.

After gutting him, I sat on a rock and studied the expanse below. Puffs of mist rose from the wet earth and were touched pink by the late sun. The only sounds were those made by crystal beads of water dripping off the bright emerald cedars. Having killed the buck clean like that, with all the world ticking so smoothly around me, I felt as alive and good as a man could.

But such bliss seldom lasts for long, and with a black wall of clouds approaching from the west, I thought I'd better get busy with the mile drag. So I left this prayer and started downhill, pulling my trophy behind me. I kept coming across very big rocks turned over by the very big bear. I didn't want to leave the deer overnight so that the bear—or anybody else—would gnaw on it. But the deer and the skies were getting very heavy, and I realized that I would have to stash the meat for the night if I expected to get to the car before dark. I pushed it under a tree and then, to keep any scavengers at bay, I pissed around the tree and hastily draped my light jacket over the deer. I headed for the car. Within a few minutes it started to rain and I thought of returning for the jacket, but the car wasn't that far off.

I was in the bottom of a canyon that fed into a larger one. Just past where they joined was where I expected the car to be. But it wasn't. By now the rain was really coming down—pushed sideways by a wind that moaned with an eerie howl. I realized a few hard facts instantly: I had little light to find the car, my flashlight was in it, and if I couldn't find the car I was in a world of hurtin'. Although I had a lighter, I wouldn't be able to build a fire, as everything was totally soaked. I might soon be facing a long night in the woods under the worst conditions imaginable.

I got scared, and with that my mind got quick and useless. I frantically searched up—and then down—the canyon. I have no idea how long or far I had gone when

I finally faced the fact that I was getting nowhere fast, and stopped. I had some luck calming myself and made a plan: as I knew the car was on a rise, and out in the open, I might be able to find it by silhouetting it against the faint skyline. But there were endless lone cedars spaced out in the fields—all about the size and color of my dark-colored SUV. I approached each one hoping against hope that it would turn into my car. It got so dark that I had to go up and actually touch the trees. But it was useless.

I needed to get out of the weather and take stock. It was too dark to find decent shelter so I got on the lee side of a big cedar. I fumbled in my pack and found my lighter. I lit part of the map, and put the rest of it under my cap to help keep my head dry. With the aid of the little torch I checked on the contents of the pack that I had so hastily grabbed that afternoon. There was not much there of use, and I placed the unnecessary baggage—rifle, binoculars, and knife—under the tree. I had the deer's liver in there also and thought it might come in handy, but only as a last resort. I had eaten the stuff raw before (it really needs to be cooked with onions) and figured I'd eat it just before the creaking of death's door. I found some flagging in the pack and tied it in the branches above the gear. I did have a warm and dry fleece jacket in there and replaced my soaked shirt with it. That felt much better.

The tree I was under left me too exposed and I knew that I needed more protection from the weather. I headed down the slope in little baby steps so as not to trip over rocks or plunge over any of the numerous cliffs that frequented the area. I made it down to the bottom of the draw and found a bigger, more protected tree to hide under. I took the arm of the shirt and swung it against the branches to get some of the water off of the tree. I then wrung the shirt out and hung it on the branches. I squatted under it and tried to make myself as small a target as possible for the cold, deadly raindrops.

Now I had time on my hands—lots of it—and I tried to fathom the situation. My mind and spirits were in OK shape. And I was still pretty dry—although water was starting to slosh in my boots. Oddly, I was having a hard time grasping the fact that, after fifty years of tromping around in the sticks, I was in serious trouble for the first time. I knew that people die of hypothermia under much pleasanter conditions than these. I remembered reading about a kid who froze to death next to a fire in summer! A fire would have thrown me into the lap of luxury. The rain pounded down, to my disbelief; after all, this was New Mexico, it must let up any minute. Too bad it wasn't snow; I could have brushed snow off myself and found dry wood and built a fire.

I knew that cold wasn't far off, because I was getting wet, and that I'd better make a plan while my mind and body were still in good working order. I could see the glow of cars on the highway to the east. I had noticed two ranches, one to the southeast and the other to the west. All three choices were roughly the same distance away—five miles. Not all that far in the daylight. I didn't know this country very well, and my map was of little use because I didn't know where I was to begin with. But I knew that there were plenty of canyons and cliffs in any five-mile hunk of the ground here. The ranch to the west was probably the best choice, because I seemed to remember the way to it looking the flattest. Plus there was a fence that ran somewhat in that direction, and I figured I could follow the straight line for part of the way. And I had been to that ranch, and even met someone coming out the gate who gave me directions. Seemed like a chap who wouldn't turn away some slobbering semblance of a human crawling up to his doorstep at 3 a.m.

Deciding to go for it, I made it about fifty feet into that brutal storm before I turned tail and shuffled back to my pitiful shelter. It was just too nasty out there—but I was getting cold here too. I groped among some nearby rocks for any hint of a cave to crawl into. I pressed and squirmed against several rocks to find any sort of overhang that might keep me dry, but with no luck. I moved my shirt to higher branches on the tree so that I could stand under it, and started to jog in place to warm up. After perhaps half an hour of this I realized that it was not keeping me ahead of the penetrating cold. My neck and back were stiffening up. I struck the lighter and looked at my watch—it was 9:30. Only ten more hours to go! Could I keep this up till sunup? The answer to that was a resounding NO, and I started to think about my kids, my friends, the woman in my life, my life.

When that line of thinking reached its inevitable conclusion, I knew that it was time to take action. After wringing out the wet shirt, I wrapped it over my forehead and draped it over my shoulders and back like a cape, and set off into the gale. The climb up to the top of the hill helped warm me up a little, but my back and neck were still stove up. When I reached the top of the hill I could see the lights of the highway and the glow of the ranches. I couldn't help but picture people all toasty and content under those near, but yet so far, lights. I was not totally sold on the west ranch, and I looked from one light to the other, trying to remember the lay of the land—wishing I had paid more attention during that glorious period known as daylight. I remember thinking, "Get it right, this could be your last big decision."

Then for some reason I turned back toward the mountain to the north and saw—right in the middle of the vast blackness—a faint light. A pinprick so dim that I doubted its existence, and thinking that my soggy mind had transferred one of the distant lights to a handier locale I turned back and forth several times to make sure it was real. The popular consensus was that it was there all right, but I couldn't for the life of me figure out what it could be. Although I hadn't seen anybody around, it might be somebody's camp.

It was sure a lot closer than those other lights, so I decided to go toward it. All that was visible underfoot were the patches of yellow grass between the black rocks, and knowing that sheer drop-offs were everywhere, I tried to stay on the grass as I went. But I still had to inch my way along, as there was about as much invisible black rock as there was yellow grass. The light grew steadily brighter. At one point, it disappeared and I went into a panic, but I backtracked until I picked it up again.

Realizing that there were trees in the way, I proceeded ever so slowly so as not to lose sight of the weak beacon. I came to a place where I had to leave the light completely to drop into an arroyo. When I came back up the other side a couple of anxious minutes later, the light was much closer and was beginning to take shape. And each step was convincing me that I was seeing my dear, sweet car. Then I could make it out—it was the dome light in my car—and I realized that I had left the door ajar a few hours ago. (Fortunately, I had bought a new battery the week before.) I yelled, I screamed, lived a thousand lives, and died a thousand deaths. I didn't know how frightened I was until then. I don't know how to explain what it was like—but I physically shuddered to the ground with relief.

I got inside and started her up. I removed the wet clothes—a tight maneuver in the driver's seat, but I refused to set one foot outside again to make taking the clothes off easier. I got the heater on full blast and found some dry clothes. I ate some absolutely delicious peanut butter and jelly, listened to Coltrane sail among the stars, and after blasting myself with an hour of jubilant heat, crawled into my down sleeping bag.

Several hours later I awoke to find the car being rocked back and forth. Maybe the big bear was trying to get in? But it was just the wind—a violent wind still loaded with rain. I was cold and wrapped myself in another blanket. I thought, "If I am this cold in here, I would not have made it to that farmhouse." As I lay there swept with gratitude, I had a dreamy vision. I pictured a trembling animal—no bigger than a grain of sand—huddled under a rock as a powerful world lashed its fury at it. The half of me that was conscious was overpowered by this image and forced the sleeping half awake so that I could experience this rare moment of true humility.

In the morning I went for the deer. The sun was shining off fresh snow on top of the mountain when I got under way. Having been so turned around the night before, I wasn't surprised to learn that the deer was not in the canyon I thought I had come down but in another one. Nobody had bothered the meat during the night, and I dragged the buck down to the main canyon. Then I spent a long time searching for the gear that I had put under the tree, with no luck. So I went back to the car, figured out what direction I had approached it from the night before, and backtracked from there.

No doubt I had been searching the wrong area all morning, but the canyon that now looked to be the obvious choice was very rugged. I had already been by it and written it off, thinking I couldn't possibly have negotiated that place in the dark. But I decided to look again and traipsed almost the length of it. I scaled a short cliff to get out, and when I reached the top, I took a look backward. And there, on the opposing side—to my amazement—was the flagged tree. Below the tree, there was a narrow opening that led to the canyon bottom where I had taken shelter. Looking over the scene, I realized I was very lucky to have found my way in and out of there, as sheer rock surrounded the place on three sides. I climbed down and sat under the tree where I had spent those cold hours and wept. How I had made it through that deadly night—and into this incredibly beautiful day—God knows.

CHAPTER TWENTY-ONE

RAISING AN ELK HUNTER

■ ■ ■

My son got his first elk license when he was eleven. He had passed his hunter safety course, and as long as he had someone—like me—to tote the heavy rifle, he was licensed to kill cow elk. This also qualified me as a guide, and as such I found him an elk to shoot at. But I'd misjudged the distance and said, "It's a long way, better hold high," and the bullet raised dust over the animal's back. Later the same day he missed one that wasn't so tough a shot. He had had a good rest but jerked the trigger, and that threw the bullet off course. Like most folks who have never shot at big game, he didn't figure on missing—how much can there be to putting an animal in the crosshairs and pulling the trigger?

This cooled him on hunting for a while, and he didn't get his next elk tag until he was sixteen. No self-respecting, macho, New Mexican teenager is going to kill a cow elk, so he got a bull license.

We had a couple of days of poor hunting in warm weather but awoke to a snow-storm on our third day. Snow forces elk down from the high country on migration trails that have been used for thousands of years. These routes efficiently take them through saddles, around mountains and cliffs, and across steep canyons, the herd increasing in size as it funnels toward its wintering grounds.

There is such a good chance of seeing elk on such a snowy morning that your senses become ultra acute. Individual snowflakes tumble down in the opaque light as you listen for the thud of hooves. Your nostrils search the passing air for the scent of elk. This is what being alive is all about—using rusty instincts that our ancestors used to outsmart this same species for thousands of years.

But modern man—this one anyway—is too scattered to keep that kind of edge for long and I was physically relieved when I realized that the elk weren't around. We made a new plan. Fresh tracks in the snow told us that we were behind a big bunch that went south during the night. So we drove to get ahead of them.

When we reached a saddle that we suspected they would cross, we stopped the jeep. Instantly we saw movement on a wooded hillside above us. We made out horns; the elk's path would take it into the open in a half second. Nick grabbed his rifle and raised it as the elk reached the opening. The animal stopped seventy-five yards away and Nick fired. The elk darted into the woods. We climbed to the spot and searched, but there was no blood, no hair, and no elk.

We were both amazed at not finding any evidence of a hit, because it was a close broadside shot. After Nick's bummer mood subsided, I told him that at least it was a clean miss. I went on to describe a horrible experience that I had had wounding a deer. It was so bad that I didn't hunt for several years, and when I reentered the field I had a truer aim. The incident had made me aware of the responsibility involved in pulling that trigger. And now, just before I send the bullet on its way, I have a better understanding of the weight of the act and, for that brief instant, the world stops. There's no breath, no thought, only the junction of the crosshairs at this moment of great intensity.

The next day we drove to the edge of a huge canyon and started glassing at first light. We saw a herd with a big bull below us, but it was too far away. Just then a shot rang out from a long way off and spooked the elk. They started running parallel to the rimrock and we tried to keep up with them by getting back from the edge—to solid ground—and jogging. After a quarter mile we went back to the edge of the canyon, but somehow those great big animals had disappeared. We figured we might as well stay put and sat about fifty yards apart. As the thrill of the chase wore off, I relaxed and hung my legs over the cliff and gazed at the endless New Mexico mountains. Dark volcanic hills stood silhouetted against the higher, snow-covered Jemez range. But I couldn't keep my eyes off the canyon below. The valley floor was, like I said earlier, too far for a shot—but directly below us, and only halfway to the bottom, there was a shelf. It was only a few acres, but at least it was in range.

It was pleasant enough, but twenty minutes had passed by without seeing anything, so I called to Nick, "Let's split." I was already on my feet and back from the edge, but my yell spooked something, because I heard a rock roll from below. I snapped a look at

Nick with his first elk

Nick. He had raised his rifle, and, as I ran over, he fired. I heard the bullet thud home. The bull was running across the middle of that tiny open shelf and I took a shot myself. I saw my bullet miss. I then jammed my gun in my fumbling excitement—so much for my moment of intensity—but Nick continued to fire. Just as the bull went over a little rise, it slipped—then stumbled at the top. It went out of view into the small arroyo and didn't come up the other side.

We stayed on the rim for a few minutes, to see if the elk would reappear—and to recapture our composure. So strange—after such a violent few seconds, all was quiet again. Did that all really just happen? Nick couldn't believe it because, while daydreaming on the cliff, he imagined a bull trotting across that little bench—exactly where it did! It took us a few minutes to find our way down through the cliff. We followed the torn-up trail to the dead bull. Nick said "Oh my God" a lot and we hugged and laughed.

This would make a nice Hollywood ending, wouldn't it? All we'd need to finish the tale would be some ecologically correct overtures: the backbreaking work of "making meat," how we made candles from the fat, moccasins from the hide, and so on.

But my readers will get their share of the bold truth. Just like with our kids, we not only get to live their victories, but their defeats as well....

A year went by and we found ourselves at the same overlook armed in the same manner, hoping for the same results. Nick had reached the all-knowing age of seventeen—when all the world was his slave and killing another elk would be a piece of cake. And sure enough, by the faint gray light of dawn, we could see three bull elk through the glasses, feeding in a hidden meadow. They were a mile off and we had to move fast in order to get close enough for a shot before they headed into the timber. But we decided that it might be better if I stayed behind on the rim to keep an eye on them. Nick disappeared into the rocks and trees below. I waited for what seemed a long time and even started to worry about my boy. I was watching the bulls graze as the sun turned the snow-covered Jemez range pink beyond them. And then a shot. I got my eye back on the spotting scope and watched two bulls run across the field. More shots. Then the running bulls made the trees and all was quiet.

But the third bull remained standing, back where everything started, with its head down, obviously hit. I waited for Nick to finish the animal off. But there was no shot, just a very sick animal standing in the field. I grew frustrated and then worried that maybe Nick had hurt himself. But then I saw him walk out into the field, heading toward the two elk that had run off and away from the wounded elk. I yelled at the top of my lungs for him to kill the wounded elk. I seethed as he continued to walk in the wrong direction, and yelled until I was hoarse. And then the event that I had been dreading happened. Instead of falling over dead, the big bull started walking toward the timber. I knew that once it was in there our chances of finding it would plummet. It walked to the fence at the edge of the meadow, stood there for a moment, gathered its strength, and finally jumped over it.

That meant the end of my usefulness on the rim, and I headed down. Watching that spectacle had made me sick with ugly adrenalin-driven emotions. And when I got to the meadow Nick was nowhere to be found. I went to where the elk had stood for so long and studied the ground. I followed the sign into the woods, but the faint blood trail gave out in a few feet. Then the tracks became lost in a maze of other tracks. I returned to the meadow and there was Nick. I flew into a rage that I'm still ashamed of. How could he let this happen? What the hell was wrong with him? Arrogant teenage idiot!

That was the first time he realized that he had even hit one of the three bulls and, between the incredible intensity of the situation, my laying all my poisonous feelings on him, and the realization of what this animal was going through, we both broke down and cried about the mess.

When we had gotten rid of some of that grief, Nick told me what happened. When he got down to the edge of the field, he only saw two elk. There was a slight rise in the field and he could only make them out from above the legs. He took good rest on a tree limb and fired. When the smoke cleared, there were two elk running across the meadow and, figuring that he had missed, he started firing at one of them as they ran by him. He started to follow them to see if he had hit the one he was shooting at. When he got out in the field a little, he thought that he had better look back to the scene of the crime. But by then he had walked below the rise in the field and couldn't see the wounded bull standing there. He still thought that there were only two elk when he shot. It was an honest mistake—but one neither one of us is likely to make again.

We looked for that elk for the next three days. We walked the timber, glassed for hours from the rimrock looking for feeding birds or any sign of the bull. Long and low work. Toward the end of this penance, Nick turned to me and said that he would go to college the following year, and not hunt elk next fall. This was a far more accessible and vulnerable boy than he had been at the beginning of the hunt. He also said that the next time he shot at such a great animal he would have a better understanding of the responsibility involved. That responsibility is what stops the world from turning—long enough for a hunter to squeeze the trigger and send off a killing shot.

Chapter Twenty-two

ZEUS—GOD OF BIRD DOGS

■ ■ ■

There is a saying in Argentina that it's been a good life if you "build a house, write a book, and plant a tree." Although the house was never finished, the books aren't best sellers, and the tree has yet to bear fruit, I've approached all three. But my list would add: "and have one great bird dog." Unlike the aforementioned semisatisfying accomplishments, Zeus was top shelf all the way.

He was an adorable black Labrador from blood so good that just the sight of a cur sneaking out the back door of the kennel compromised the litter's pedigree. With their nobility in question, he and his brothers and sister were disdainfully given away. I naturally chose the most rambunctious male, figuring that it would take a headstrong soul to put up with all the cuddling and cooing that he would get at home and still be ballsy enough to hunt. So he lived a double life: sweet pet at home, savage beast afield.

He was never properly trained—just tossed in the deep water to sink or swim. But I hunted a lot, so that started when he was just three months old. His first assignment was the capture of a wounded mallard drake. The duck was flapping about and once the little puppy spotted it he ran over and grabbed on. The bird tried to fly and lifted some of the pup's feet right off the ground! This caused some ineffectual puppy growls, but he never let go; and since Zeus was a couple of ounces heavier than the duck, the pair stayed earthbound and we collected the duck before it flapped the puppy to death.

A year later at the same lake Zeus and I got two geese—without my ever firing a shot. We were walking along some thick grass and the dog jumped in there as if on a mission. He returned a couple of minutes later carrying a live Canada goose. After handing me the bird he turned around and dove back in the thick cover and brought me a second one! They had been wounded by someone else and the incredible nose of the dog kept those birds from going to waste.

After a few seasons Zeus learned that wounded ducks dive down in one place to resurface elsewhere. It was funny to watch him figure this out—because at first he'd just stare at the hole in the water that the departed duck had made with a quizzical expression on his face. Over time he discovered that they often swim a considerable distance underwater, and began to search the banks downstream of where a duck had dived. Once I wounded a duck that never swam to the bank but kept eluding the dog by diving. I couldn't finish it off because of the close proximity of duck and dog. Just when Zeus was ready to grab the bird it would dive again. The dog got more and more aggressive and would submerge himself a little farther each time. Once he even spit some tail feathers out of his mouth. He finally dove right in after the bird and was down there for what seemed a long time. All got quiet on the pond, and I started to worry. And then he blasted through the surface like a submarine full of air—duck in mouth.

The other incredible waterfowl retrieve that I will always remember was of four greater Canada geese at the same time. Yes, four at one time.

Before I explain, I will start with the acquisition of those geese, as that is a pretty interesting story, too. We were hunting a remote part of a canyon and spotted the birds from the rim. We made our way down the gorge and then snuck up as close as we could to them, using trees for cover. But the trees ran out and we couldn't go any farther without being seen. It was in the morning and the sun was still behind the canyon wall and had not yet reached the birds. We were on the east side of the river and the birds were resting on the west bank, and they would be in the sunlight before us. So I thought that they might be blinded by the first rays of the bright sun when it hit their eyes—and maybe not see us approaching from the still-dark east side.

It was a very long wait as we watched the sunlight creep down toward the birds. When the light finally reached them, the dog and I got up and walked straight at them. We were right across the narrow river and they still hadn't seen us. Zeus couldn't restrain himself and swam across. When he was just about to bite one on the toe they took off. I shot two, which the dog promptly retrieved. While he was attending to the fetching,

Zeus fetches a mallard in Colorado.

I was blowing on the goose call; the flock turned around and passed right overhead, and I shot two more.

Four greater Canada geese weigh in at fifty pounds, and although I was sure looking forward to putting them in the smoker, I wasn't so happy about getting them down the canyon and then up the trail. But I had an idea. The river didn't seem too fast here, so I would just tie their necks together and float the raft of dead birds down to the trail. I took a cord and tied it around their necks and sent them into the flow. Everything was just fine for the first half mile, and my pace walking was faster than theirs floating. But as the going got rougher, the water got faster, and the flock started preceding me downriver.

This is one rugged mother of a canyon and the only way out is by trail; and our trail was adjacent to where the canyon walls came right down to the river, thereby cutting off access downstream. If they floated beyond that point I would never get them. So I was scrambling over huge rocks trying to catch up. But I fell behind, and the only thing I could think to do was explain the situation to Zeus and see if he could pull a Lassie for me.

I'm sure you old-timers remember how Timmy would explain a complicated situation to Lassie, draw her a little map in the dust, and then give her a "You can do it, girl." She'd respond with a "woof," then head over the hill and save the baby that had just fallen into a cesspool. Now I'm not the gullible type, and I never believed that Lassie could understand a damn word that Timmy was saying, but once I laid down the facts to my dog, he ran downriver, swam out to the birds, and pulled the fifty pounds of 'em straight in to shore! True, it was the far shore, and I had to cross the river to get at them, but when I arrived, there was Zeus treading water and holding the flotilla.

(I shot some geese down there this year—and, being some twenty-five years smarter, cut the meat off the birds and put it in my pocket for the hike out—da!)

But Zeus's main strength was with quail. Most labs are shaped like muskrats, but Zeus had long legs and he bounced mightily across the New Mexico desert. We hunted below Truth or Consequences mostly, and it was back in the glory days when it was possible to find a lot of birds. I had already learned that his senses were a lot better than mine, but I was a bit too proud to admit that the dog was smarter than me, too!

In that southern desert, in winter, the Gambel's quail can be found in large coveys. Sometimes you would spend half a day before you would see them, but then you'd bust up a gang of a hundred or more. Your shooting would be secured for the rest of the day if you knew where the birds went after the covey rose. But as that country is all arroyos, mesas, and brush, it isn't easy to mark them down. They usually sail over a ridge, and it is tough to figure which way they went.

This is where the Labrador's final card—his intelligence—came through, because somehow he knew where to look. It wasn't by smell or sight, just from lots of experience. After a covey would flush over a ridge, we'd make it up to the top as quickly as we could, and once on top the wonder dog would stop and survey the area, and then we'd take off in whatever direction he chose. (I was a stubborn guy at that time in my life, but I wanted my birds, and he had to prove over and over that he knew better than me.) We'd head straight over to some little draw, and he would start routing those quail out of there one by one.

I ran a little trap line during those times of high fur prices. I set one trap just next to the Hondo creek on the narrow road that runs toward Taos Ski Valley. When I went to check the trap one morning it was gone and all that was left was the sign of a big commotion. The coyote had run off with the trap and I didn't have a clue as to where. So I returned home for my bloodhound, Zeus. When I had shown him the spot, he took off in a beeline straight up the mountain, and before I knew it there was a hell of a commotion going on up there. I started up as fast as I could, but by the time I reached the steep ridge above the creek, the ruckus had switched back below me. So around I turned and down the hill I flew. And there in the middle of the road at 9 a.m. were mighty Zeus and one mean-ass coyote going at it. There were cars full of skiers lined up as the fur flew. Imagine the horror on the faces of the onlookers! The coyote jumped in the creek and I shot it—it died along with my trapping career.

Zeus wasn't too friendly with other New Mexico critters either. We lived on the edge of the forest, and he took it upon himself to eradicate every nasty varmint in the Sangre de Cristo! They say that the more intelligent a dog is the more trouble it has with skunks and porcupines, because once it gets stuck or stunk it doesn't forget and stays at war for a lifetime. Zeus once came home with a mouth full of quills and stinking of skunk! Any personal sacrifice needed to terminate one of those animals was worth it for Zeus. I still have scars on my elbows from when I would try to hold him down so that my wife could yank the quills out with pliers.

He wasn't too keen on bears either, and there was one grouse-hunting area that had so many that we had to keep Zeus out of there for fear that he would exterminate them. I never actually saw him face to face with a bear, but there would be a whole lot of hissing, growling, and howling off in the trees whenever he got into an argument with one.

All this high livin' took its toll on old Zeus, and by the time he was ten years old he had half a tail, sliced-up ears, and a permanent limp. But he still knew where the quail were, could see a duck coming before I would, and kept the neighborhood free of skunks and porcupines.

I have always felt that the quote "dog is God spelled backward" was a tawdry saying, but in my eyes it just might be applicable to Zeus, who was named for a god—and rightly so. Zeus God Dog was probably his full name. We never checked because the bastard's papers weren't in order.

Coming out of the fog

CHAPTER TWENTY-THREE

FIFTY

■ ■ ■

My fiftieth birthday looms just ahead. I think I would get a better view of the grue-some event from someplace far afield than from the tightly wrapped tourist town I live in. So I grab the over and under, take my son's Lab, Sheba, and hit the road.

Off before daylight, we pass through a high New Mexico valley at dawn. The cold and snow have forced the elk out into the open, and they stand sideways in the first light, taking in the warmth. Their coats turn pink as the red rays soak into their yellow bodies. Having one in the freezer allows me to watch them with a relaxed eye.

As I continue, memories also emerge from familiar scenery. I drive by a ranch that I hunted elk and deer on for several seasons, and remember the hunts fondly. The truth is that there was more backbreaking work than hunting—slogging through mud and snow, getting stuck, then dragging, skinning, and butchering the animal. Other hunts flash by: I pass a valley where a gobbler strutted in to my call; then there was that deer I tried to shoot. . . . But enough of this, now where was I going? Oh yeah, to Spanish Lake for geese.

Well shy of the lake I see several bald eagles in a little group of trees. I wonder why they are so far from water. When I reach the lake the answer is obvious, as there isn't any water—it's all ice. Which has of course sent the geese off. There are some ducks in the ditch below the lake, though. And what a sight it makes: the jet-black Lab carrying the greenhead through new snow and sparkling subzero fog, the great Rocky Mountains floating above it all in the background. Twenty years ago, in this same ditch, my trusty Lab Zeus retrieved his first mallard. My mind's eye sees the little three-month-old pup being just about taken aloft when he latched onto the wounded duck.

I'd heard about some quail an hour to the east. I'm always interested in new country, and fewer distractions from the past should make me a better hunter. So I aim toward Texas on one of those wonderfully open New Mexico highways, so lonely that you can stop where you like and pee down the center stripe.

When sparse pasture gives way to grass and brush, it's time to stop and have a look. Sure enough, there are some quail tracks in the sand. Sheba and I look all over, finally finding them at the windmill—where we should have looked in the first place. The quail are running around some old rusted ranch junk as I top the rise. They conveniently get up by the half covey; the first bunch leaves from under the fender of an old truck and the rest burst out of a tangle of wire. This allows me to reload the double and get off lots of lead. It nets me only one bird, but I've got the others marked down.

As anyone who has hunted scaled quail can attest, they are part roadrunner and marking them down may not mean a lot. But in this thin pasture I jog from bush to bush and manage to find a few more to miss and a couple to collect. We cross another covey before heading to town and sack up a couple more birds, but it is the next day's hunt that I will remember.

The blue morning finds me pulling up to a deserted farmhouse. The place sits on a little rise of land. Elms shade a bent gray barn and a windmill squeaks in the faint breeze. As I examine the antelope tracks at the water, a large covey of quail gets up. I manage a double as they rise, and Sheba finds them quickly. The rest of the covey fans out in tall grass punctuated by brilliant green yucca. Even scaled quail will hold tight in this thick stuff. I urge Sheba to hunt, and when the big quail rise up, the perfect lighting slows them enough so that I can hit them. In fact, I end up quitting the covey so as not to annihilate the lot.

I walk around for a while, peacefully bored, and find a dried-up frog and a 45-million-year-old fossil. Time for something else, and this is supposed to be a goose hunt. I've seen several flocks in the distance and I figure they are headed to the lake I see on the map. It's twenty or so miles off, but I don't get far before I see a big crowd of them in a cornfield. I leave Sheba in the car and head out low through the cornstalks. I think to myself that I have again, somehow, arrived at the right place at the right time. It's late in the afternoon, and they're milling the air making that wonderful Canadian racket. A bunch swarms toward me, and out of the corner of my eye, I see them coming directly over. I remain still, and then raise up to shoot. I miss with the modified barrel, but then one folds when I fire the full choke. I pick up what seems like a very large bird after the quail. I watch the rest of them fade off into the night.

It's a happy drive to my motel as I picture my fiftieth birthday starting at dawn in the cornfield. I think the geese will return, but I'm not positive. Incredibly, before bed I read, in a goose-hunting story in an outdoor magazine that I brought with me, that the creatures always return in the morning to the field they left the night before!

It's "happy birthday to me" as I waddle out in the dark, wrapped in enough garments to lie in the snow for a couple of hours. I'm surprised to find that I have packed a white blanket to camouflage myself in. The wait seems long, but finally, what looks at first like just another wavy thin cloud above the pastel horizon, honks. They're coming straight at me with wings set—but they pass to the right. The next couple of bunches give me shots, but getting up into firing position (with blanket and all) is messy and slow. I decide to go and hide behind the wheel of a sprinkler system a ways off. It's perfect: there are even narrow holes in the wheel that I can look through to see the approaching birds. Except now they are coming from every which way, and I jump from one side of the wheel to the other before I decide on holding out for a group that's coming straight at me, flying low in the rising wind. Their course continues and I stand up and fire, and one crashes to earth. This doesn't seem to have deterred the others, as additional waves shift this way and that. I try to steer some closer with a honk of my own. It seems to be working when suddenly one calls from straight overhead. I wheel around and another Canada goose bites the red dust.

This being about as many greater Canadas as a relatively sane man would want to pluck, I pack it in. So satisfied am I with all this that I don't even bother to chase a covey of quail that I flush on the way back to the car. (I do, however, casually check to see if I have any number eight shot. Lest you fear that fifty has found me too sane!)

I've got a birthday dinner planned with the kids and old friends, so I'm heading back home on that lonely highway. It's a reflective drive with piano notes floating inside the jeep. Thoughts and emotions come and go, as do the hawks on fence posts. I beep at a herd of antelope. The sound takes an amount of time to reach them and then they raise their heads. I easily come to one conclusion. Fifty is not so bad—at least the first few hours.

I was bitching about it to my friend Laurie and she pointed out that this is it, time for the good life. We finally know a little something and can perhaps discriminate as to the proper time and place to apply it. The struggle to reach some higher, firmer ground is not so arduous. We may not often be standing on the hill, but at least we have some idea where it is. As for me, I've no reason to complain. I don't hear Laurie whining, and she's in a wheelchair. I watched my two closest friends die painful, lingering deaths in the past year. They valued each jarring tick of the clock, each struggling breath, with an appreciation that I seldom have.

I drop back to earth to continue my investigations, heading down a long dirt road. The sight of two bull elk lounging in someone's pasture startles me. They look out of place here, twenty miles from the mountains. They have similar racks, tall, spindly

4X5. I stop and wave, but only one acknowledges my presence by getting up. They're jaded after hunting season and tired after hiking through the deep snow. Just as I leave them—to rejoin the main highway home—two meadowlarks take flight and fly beside the truck. Their wings beat a few times, then stop, their yellow and brown bodies fall toward earth, and then their wings carry them up again. A never-ending cycle. We bob down the road this way for what seems like a long time.

Always release dangerous animals with care.

PART VI

COLLATERAL DAMAGE

CHAPTER TWENTY -FOUR

ANIMALS

■ ■ ■

The first place I ever flung a fly was in the swamp in back of my childhood home. And my first creature on a fly wasn't a fish, but a frog. And technically it actually wasn't a fly that caught it, but a piece of red yarn attached to a safety pin. This was the best a five-year-old Davy Crockett could come up with, as I had no means of getting to a proper body of water, to catch a proper fish with a proper fly. But when Froggy unrolled his way-long tongue to inhale my artificial, we both got hooked. That was fifty years ago, and since then I've gotten to fish better water and hook onto some pretty interesting animals, items, and even a few fish.

In the hopes of helping young fly fishers understand what they can expect in "collateral hookups" in their fishing future, I have computed the "rate of frequency." These statistics were derived from intricate notes kept over the years on the probability of hooking various animals, objects, and world records.

Also lumped in here are bizarre incidents involving fish and various combinations of all of the above. But let me give you a "for instance" of how these odds work—your frogs, for instance, are easy to apprehend and it takes about three casts to hook your average frog. Keep in mind that that's sight fishing for frogs, as blind fishing for frogs has a dismal success rate. I hope these numerical projections will help an angler in deciding what collateral species and objects are likely to come his way over the course of time.

At Casa Blanca Lodge on the Yucatán peninsula, I got to fish for a larger reptile than the aforementioned frog. This pristine area is one of the few places where it is possible to fish for bonefish, tarpon, permit, and snook all in the same day. And once you make shore, you may add the iguana to your "grand slam" list. If you've ever "fished frog," you have it made, because the experienced reptiler knows that all it takes is to tie a little piece of cloth to the end of your leader and cast it out close to the quarry. Make sure that it is hookless, because the animal will most certainly charge it, and you don't really want to catch the thing. Pulling the fly away from it will create even greater sport, because that will make the iguana go on a tongue-flicking rampage. And sensing the hubbub, his companions will quickly come running from the jungle. This activity will then draw other anglers from the cocktail lounge and soon iguanas and anglers will be all-a-blur on the lawn. (The frequency for iguana takes is high—1 in 5.5 casts—if you let 'em take it, that is.)

Fortunately, most nontargeted animals are fangless and friendly—often of the feathered clan: duck, kingfisher, dipper, tern, swallow, nighthawk, seagull, dove. Dangerous game includes your alligators, your larger muskrats, dogs, beavers, cows (especially your bull cows), and your larger bats (your vampire bats are to be avoided). It is not recommended to fish for such dangerous game.

But I have fished for gator, and a caiman in Brazil; it was sitting under a tree and I managed to sling a cast over a branch above it. The big fly was not snagged or hooked, and I could raise and lower it by pulling on the line. It was dangling directly over the caiman, and I teased the animal into leaping up and chasing the fly. I figured that if he actually caught it, the fly would be quickly parted from the leader by the lizard's abundant toothage. So I would pull it out of his reach, but as his frustration rose, so did the extent of his leapage, and he finally made a wild jump and caught the fly. As expected, he instantly absconded with it. (Although I lack in-depth statistics here, I'm guessing the frequency for caiman takes is almost 1 in 1 attempts.)

I've hooked all manner of material goods but just your run-of-the-mill stuff: flies ending up in cans and bottles, old shoes, a couple of pairs of underwear. Never anything with value or esteem, but I did hear of someone who was giving casting instruction in some nasty water in Denver who came up with a foot-long dildo. Apparently the twelve-incher wasn't hooked at the pointy end but amidships, forcing the battle to last for some time. (Frequency for dildo hooking is 1 in 181,756.2.)

It is not uncommon to lasso a fish. (When I say "not uncommon" I mean, compared to something like dildo fishing.) As my calculations reveal that about one in 9,002 fish is caught this way—not by hooking the fish's flesh, but by lassoing it with a loop of leader. (This is how Native Americans in my area of New Mexico are said to have fished, back in the day—by sneaking up on a sighted fish and slipping a noose over its neck. But, just like us catch-and-release nuts, it is also reported that they didn't care about actually eating fish. So it's doubtful that they bothered to calculate the probability of success—because if they knew how dismal their odds were, they might never have gone fishing.)

Another rarity is catching a fish that has had a previous brush with another angler and has line already hanging from it. I once caught a trout when my fly caught the loop of a snelled hook that was protruding about three inches from the trout's mouth. (The rate of frequency for this event is about 1 in 113,000 casts—although I have witnessed line hanging from a fish's anus, I have yet to make an anal apprehension, and will withhold speculation on frequency rates of hooking trout from that end.)

Another good catch is recovering a fly that you have lost in a particular fish. (I don't mean just finding any old fly in a fish—that is relatively commonplace with a 1 in 1,354 occurrence rate.) I can recall two of these events—both in the Rio Grande in New Mexico. The first occurred one evening when I was fishing the spring caddis hatch by Manby Hot Springs. The fishing was very good and so it was my second night in a row on the same stretch of water. The evening before I had caught, released, and broken off many fish. The fish got busy the next evening when the sun went off the water, and I released a nice trout by removing a size fourteen Henryville special from its mouth. But when I let it go I found that it was still on the line. I realized that the fly in my hand did not have a leader attached to it, and I reeled the trout in once more and released the second Henryville special from the other side of its jaw.

Another time, also on the Rio Grande, I spotted a nice riser for my client. I figured that we wouldn't need to match the tiny dry it was feeding on because the trout was close to the grassy bank and probably used to eating grasshoppers. The fellow caught the fish, but when he got it in he lifted it up by the leader and the fat fifteen-incher broke off and fell back in the drink. That was the only hopper like that I had, so I wasn't too happy about losing it. We fished our way back through there an hour later and he cast to a rising fish and it turned out that he hooked the same rainbow, so we retrieved the errant hopper from it.

I'm going to let you in on my calculation process, lest you think I was making these numbers up! Here's how you figure it—this event has happened to me 2 times and I have fished 100 days a year for 40 years and have made approximately 10 casts per minute, times 60 minutes = 3,600 casts per day, times 100 days per year = 360,000, times 40 years = 14,400,000. That makes one in 14 million attempts—but it has happened twice, so one in 7 million casts would be your number. Note that this is a round figure, so that you—the layman—can follow the math.

On occasion, the fish that an angler is after will also be the one that another fish is after (1 in 876). This tends to be exciting, because the second fish is always much larger than the first. This is a more common occurrence in the salt, because the laws of the sea apply there: big fish eat smaller fish, period! There are no silly bugs for the fish to eat, like your pansy trout so delicately dine on—meat rules. On Christmas Island I had just hooked a bonefish, but my guide and I had just seen a shark and were concerned that the shark would hit the bonefish. As this was one of many bones that I had caught in the same spot, all the action would make the sharks and 'cudas in the vicinity start salivating. The hooked bonefish was traveling at the set high speed of its standard run; then it suddenly went into warp mode. We guessed that it was being chased by the shark, and then there was a thud as the shark hit the boney. (Frequency of shark attack on hooked bonefish is 1 in 137—but you have to make 876 casts to hook each bonefish, and then play 137 of them to have any hopes of experiencing this event. So you have to be in this for the long haul, because your true frequency is 137 x 876 = 120,012 casts.)

But the shark didn't bite through the line, or break it, and I could feel its bulk on there. I started to bring it in, but the line went slack. And then we saw the line that was way out yonder looping around and coming toward us, and we knew the fish was still on. All of a sudden they appeared—bonefish protruding from shark jaws—about twenty feet in front of us. And then we saw what was making the shark swim so fast, too—a thirty-five-pound trevally was squared off with the shark and trying to steal this very popular bonefish.

They looked like a couple of dogs fighting over a bone (your regular bone that is, not your bonefish). The trevally would rush in and try to grab the fish, but the shark would turn away, blocking the effort with its body. The guide and I were frozen stiff by this spectacle, but when we regained our composure we realized that we had a big popper hooked up to a large fly rod in the boat just a few feet away. He ran over and got it and then we switched rods and I slapped the giant fly down near the fired-up trevally. He grabbed it instantly (rate of frequency of takes in such a scenario is high) and I set the hook hard, but into dead weight that didn't budge an inch. The considerable pressure that I applied to the rod seemed to have little effect on the big trevally, and for a few seconds he returned to squabbling with the shark over the bonefish!

Then the threesome of fish took off for the deep blue. The guide and I were hysterical by now and we really didn't mind the line parting on both rigs as the school went over the coral reef. After all, we had had the best of it.

We had seen a very large barracuda close by also and speculated afterward what it would have been like if he had gotten into the rumble; the 'cuda would have no doubt kicked their fishy asses. There are some bad ones around Christmas Island, and in fact my brother Jackson was on the boat that caught the current world record barracuda. It was eighty-five pounds and taken on a fly. (Calculating the odds of catching a world record requires an exceptionally broad perspective, as one must figure how many fishermen there are in areas where 'cuda live to start—about half the world's oceans—and then estimate the number of casts each fisherman makes in a lifetime. Then multiply a fisherman's lifetime of casts by the number of fishermen. That number is too big to print, and admittedly my thinking may be a tad faulty, but suffice it to say that the odds of hooking a dildo are superior to those of reeling in a world record.)

Chapter Twenty-five

HUMANS

■　■　■

You've seen that cartoon with the sandwich lying by the side of the ocean; the beach walker casually picks it up, and when he takes a nibble he is yanked into the sea by means of a nearly invisible line. This strikes a deep cord in us humans because our conceded position in the food chain makes us karmically subject to being hooked ourselves.

Justly, the first person I ever caught was myself. I was probably only eight or nine years old and bass fishing by boat. I was casting a monster bass plug, and leaving too much line out, and when I ripped a vicious cast I sank the big treble hook in the back of my head—wow! Talk about coming up short. My fishing companion tried to remove the plug, but my scalp is so tough that he couldn't get it out. As we were far from shore, and the fishing being pretty good, I chose to simply wear the thing until later. I discovered that my thick scalp is quite insensitive, and as there was no pain to emit reminders to that little fisherman's brain only an inch away, I pulled another "bonehead" move hours later when I absentmindedly reached back to see what was jiggling in my head and impaled my hand on the other hook!

Since then I've hooked myself a hundred times, but the one I remember most occurred, surprisingly, indoors. I had been tying flies in the living room one winter, and when there are that many hooks around they are gonna end up where they don't belong. While walking barefoot across the living room I hooked the bottom of my foot. It wouldn't have been that big a deal, except the hook was also attached to the carpet, meaning I was attached to the carpet, smack dab in the middle of the room. I couldn't see or get at the hook; I needed something or someone to help free me.

I hobbled around in the allowed radius, panicked like a coyote in a trap, and, being

Sandwich, anyone?

prone to the dramatic, realized that I could starve to death, as the phone and fridge were far away. I looked over at the fly-tying bench and saw my ever-so-efficient wire cutters sitting there ready to be of service—but they were out of reach in a jar with other tools. I painfully contorted myself to reach it—but no luck. (Did I mention that I was howling like a coyote, too?) I needed something to help me reach the tool, and took my shirt off, thinking that I might be able to sling it over there and knock the jar off the table. But the shirt wasn't much of a fishing tool, so I tried my belt. After a number of casts I successfully knocked the bucket of tools from the table. When it hit the floor the wire cutters took a lucky bounce. With a few more belt casts, and a long, agonizing reach, I got hold of the cutters and mercifully cut myself free.

Fish vs. man

I've snagged a goodly number of other fishermen, too. Once, when I was intent on demonstrating to a client how to sight fish a particular trout, I got snagged on something behind me and yanked a couple of times, real fast, so the fly wouldn't get attached to the tree I presumed it had lighted in. The fish I was after was hard to see, and I didn't want to take my eyes off it, so when the tugging didn't work I asked my fisherman—over my shoulder—what I was hooked on. As I got no response, I yanked again. Nothing gave, so I turned my head and was shocked to see that my fisherman was not where I had thought; having changed position, he had put himself in the line of fire, and was well hooked in the throatal area. And not simply hooked: there was a wrap-and-a-half of leader around his neck to boot! All that tugging I had been doing had tightened the noose so that his head was red, his mouth gaped, and his eyes bugged out in horror.

If you think the teacher is bad, well, some of my clients' casts have put them at far greater risk than the fish they were after—and sometimes they hooked themselves in impossible places. One couple I fished with caught each other in the same place at the same time—right in the middle of each other's backs. Another gal I guided made such wild strokes with the rod that she somehow managed to hook the inside of her nose. This refined banker's wife walked up to me with a lace hanky over her nose. The hanky was surrounded by a red face and the cloth was lifted, with reserve, to reveal a number sixteen Royal Wulff buried inside her right nostril. Before her companions arrived to compound her embarrassment, I removed the obstruction with the aid of my handy hemostats, handy for extracting flies from deep inside a trout's mouth or a maiden's nose.

Sometimes you start out fighting a fish and end up attached to a fisherman. My son, Nick, was guiding on the upper Rio Grande here in New Mexico and had a young client hook a large and robust cutbow that took off racing down the tumbling rapids. The only thing to do was follow the fleeing fish, and the guide's job is to be below the client to free the line if it gets tangled and net the beast before anyone drowns. Nick was slipping over boulders and plummeting down cataracts as the boy's father and brother brought up the rear, rescuing stuff that came floating out of the submerged guide's pockets. The fish holed up in some deep water and wouldn't budge, so Nick grabbed the leader to try and hand-line the lunker up to the net. But the hook sprang loose, and since he had his hand around the leader, the fly instantly sank into Nick's finger.

The client was upstream and figured he still had the fish hooked, because the tension was never interrupted. Nick gave a spirited yell at the point of penetration, but in the thrill of the moment amid the crashing of the river, the fisherman misinterpreted the hollering and hauled even harder on the rod. Nick looked back at the kid—who had already lost a couple of big fish—and seeing the expression of excitement and hope on the boy's face, dreaded telling him that his lunker had escaped. So he voluntarily stayed hooked for a moment. But when the fisherman and his entourage arrived, there was no fish to be presented, just a dripping guide wading to shore with a fly in his finger—left with about as much dignity as the beach walker who ate the sandwich at the beginning of this little tale.

Chapter Twenty-six

BIG FOR ITS SIZE

■ ■ ■

During the process of preparing the preceding ditty for publication, we encountered two more odd hookups. The first happened to a first-time fly fisher named Megan Dunlap. She was under the fine tutelage of guide Christina Streit. And as is normally the case when one of my guides gets to work, it wasn't long before Megan was fast to a fish. I was just downstream with another client, but quickly moved in the gals' direction when I noticed the pronounced bend in Megan's rod. We usually have to tell beginners to increase the pressure on the fish, but this wasn't necessary as her rod was literally bent over double. I yelled, "Go easy, that is the first trout of your life and it's a whale—don't lose it!"

I got hold of my huge net as I jogged upstream, but I needn't have rushed because the fish was not budging from its midstream position. Chrissy was telling Megan to apply the pressure from different angles, but nothing seemed to move the fish. And then all of a sudden the trout hit the surface, and instead of the great splashing of a lunker we saw only the slight commotion of a nine-inch trout! Disappointed though we were, we quickly agreed that this was, ounce for its very few ounces, the strongest fish ever. And although Megan continued to yank like mad the fish only continued to flip and flop in place—way out in midstream.

So I hiked up my waders and went out to try and capture the little beast. When I had finally made my way through the strong currents, I reached way out and netted the fish. I attempted to scoop it out of the drink, but the nine-inch fish was so big for its size that I couldn't lift it. So I waded closer to get more leverage to extract this wonder trout—and that is when I saw not only Megan's line, but another very thick line as well. And when I pulled on that line I discovered that it was fastened to the

Fishermen have lied about their catches since the dawn of time.

bottom of the river! We freed both lines and returned the fish to the river better off for the encounter.

Although it would seem likely that the fly had snagged onto the line itself, then slid up and caught in the mouth of the staked fish, this was not the case, for the hook at the end of the tethered line was down the gullet of the fish. Megan's fly was stuck in a corner of the fish's mouth, and appeared to have just been eaten.

Just a month after that, one of Nick's clients broke off two flies on what appeared to be a good fish. Nick found two more of the same flies and retied the dry/dropper setup. He had his client continue fishing the pool, and the fellow was soon in a tussle with a rather large trout. When they finally got the fish in hand, they were amazed to see their trailing fly was hooked onto the trailing fly of the rig that was lost just a few minutes before! (Picture two flies that are exactly the same hooked onto each other at the bend.) The dry fly from the first rig—the hand fly—was the one that was hooked in the fish.

To the reader's relief, I will restrain myself from reciting the odds of successfully fishing for such "tethered trout." But give it a go. You might catch a few thousand fish— among other things—on the way.

Getting towed to the honey hole at Eagle Nest, New Mexico

CHAPTER TWENTY-SEVEN

ICE FISHIN' AT EAGLE NEST

■ ■ ■

Since this warm winter hasn't produced enough ice at Eagle Nest to support all you die-hard fishermen, I thought I'd tell this little story to remind you about the good ole days before global warming spoiled the fun.

Years ago my son, Nick, a guy named Mike, and I slid our gear across a mile of frozen lake—out to Eagle Nest's famous "Honey Hole." The fish were unimpressed with our efforts and wouldn't eat. Slow fishin' is boring, but slow ice fishing—with its white cold—is extra so. The first to fade was eight-year-old Nick. Slumped over his hole in the ice, he appeared to be closing in on unconsciousness. He barely had a hold on his rod, and since it was sticking right down in the hole, I got worried that the spinning gear was going for a swim. Just as I started to say something, it slid out of his fingers, through the two feet of ice, and on into the drink.

We attempted a salvage operation by rigging a triple hook and jigging for the gear in the fifteen-foot-deep water. It seemed as if it would be easy to latch onto the rod,

To keep from getting cold while ice fishing, think warm thoughts.

because it and its appendages—the eyes, the reel, and the line—would be straight below us. We sent a snag hook to search the depths. We must have tried for an hour— with no luck.

As we were now a rod short, one of us simply fished with a hand line, which works perhaps better than a rod anyway. The fish finally came out of their depression and started eating like mad. One of us even caught a giant twenty-two-inch rainbow (I forget which one of us—it must not have been me, or my memory would be sharper on the subject). We had several holes drilled and we busily moved from one to another in our excitement. The lost rod was a thing of the past. Then one of us (I forget who again) started to reel up something that wasn't a fish. We looked around and realized that this was indeed the hole that the rod sank in. And by God there it came, tip first, right out of the hole! What was truly amazing was how it was hooked. The little single bait hook had managed to find its way through the last and smallest of the rod's eyes, the 1/4 inch diameter tiptop!

We got it out of the water with the awe that a salvager must feel at finding a sunken Spanish treasure. Not because we had recovered the twenty dollars worth of gear, but because fishing is about chances, hopes, and odds. When you seriously beat those odds it creates one of those "it was this big" stories that we fishermen love to tell. Here was one that could be "resurfaced" into old age.

After our wonder subsided, we realized that a lot of line had been pulled out of the submerged reel. We put Nick to reeling it in, and before long we realized, by God, there was a fish at the end of the drowned rig! Soon we had one more trout flopping on the ice. We never figured out whether the fish pulled the rod out of the sleepy kid's hands or if it had eaten the bait during the rod's patient stay on the bottom.

Could this be the elusive Super Fly?

PART VII

WHICH WAY'S UPSTREAM?

CHAPTER TWENTY-EIGHT

THE LEGEND OF SUPER FLY

■ ■ ■

Taos Fly Shop's reign of renown ran from 1980 to 1988. After a hiatus of sixteen years, it reopened in 2004 at its last known whereabouts—308B Paseo Del Pueblo Sur. Here's a bit of history about Taos's first fly shop—and its infamous proprietor, Super Fly.

Taos Fly Shop actually had two previous locations, both on the main drag in the old Sleeping Boy Building on the corner of Este Es Road. The shop moved to its current location after a vehicle drove into the building late one Saturday night. (Further reading might lead one to suspect that one of the Taos Fly Shop gang was the invader, but this is not the case.)

Other unfortunate happenings collided with Taos Fly Shop's success. It opened about the same time that molybdenum was in high demand and Molycorp, in Questa, New Mexico, was making a big underground move to get ore. That intense mining virtually killed the fine fishery on the lower Red River. And, of even greater consequence, the mighty Rio Grande, from its junction downstream with the polluted Red, could not sustain trout over a foot long.

The prosperity of the fly shop was also limited because the proprietor, known only as Super Fly, was an unreliable rapscallion. The "Gone Fishing" sign was often in the window, and if you got into the shop there was another sign suggesting you make your stay brief. This sign, which stated: "You here again?—another half hour shot," was there because fly-fishing riffraff, groupies, and wannabes were forever hanging out. The sign was, of course, ignored, and low-life anglers littered the place. These guys went mostly by aliases, like Wild in the Streets, Wild Wags, and one fellow named Tribe, who made daily stops with a stolen bottle of "Lucy" stuck in his drawers.

Because Super Fly was often out on some fishy mission, your salesperson was likely to be Richard, the jazz singer. Since he had never fished a day in his life, the poet/singer's fly recommendations were based on the artistic qualities of the flies' names. "Try an egg sucking leach, humphy, or poundmeister," he loved to say. Super Fly would try to set him on track by leaving a list of flies that were working, but if he considered the names bland he simply made up new ones. "They're taking the blue bellied bivisible and the Harvard lackey," he'd say.

Of course nothing could surprise the gang of "fly-fishing thugs"; but things went on inside that sometimes offended or mystified real clients. I have a hard time believing some of the things that Super Fly did, but old friends and clients tell of so many odd incidents that I find it difficult to dismiss them all. Last year I heard a story from some folks who had come into the shop way back when; they said that they had arrived just as Super Fly was whipping up a combination of beaver and hare's ear fur for the mighty poundmeister fly. This was done in a blender. As it whirled, the air filled with hair—and the poor souls were sneezing and coughing. When they asked Super Fly why he didn't have a top on the blender, he simply stated, "It doesn't need a top."

I asked one guy who worked there what he remembers of the olden days, and he said his favorite story occurred one morning just after he opened the shop. Super Fly pulled up in a red Cadillac convertible with several other "fishermen." The gang was sitting among a tangled mass of rods and reels and they told him that they had been fishing all night and were back in town to get supplies and "tie up some flies." Super Fly proceeded to sit at the fly-tying bench and whip up some fly that "looked like a bunch of crap on a hook." He said that when Super Fly got up, he knocked over a box with a thousand hooks, and the gang proceeded to crawl around and pick them up.

Super Fly escape vehicle?

Apparently some of them were spent from the long night of "fishing," and being so close to the floor put them in a restful mood. Soon, a couple of them were fast asleep. When tourists walked in soon thereafter, they quickly did an about-face rather than step over these fly-fishing thugs. This was quite the spectacle for Jhara, the seventeen-year-old farm boy from west Texas who had thought of fly fishermen as tweed wearing, pipe smoking gentlemen.

No doubt the reader has the impression that professionalism was lacking at the Taos Fly Shop. But, in its way, excellence abounded when it came to putting people and fish together. This is where Hall of Fame guide Taylor Streit made a name for himself, and many Taoseños got their first fly rod or learned to tie flies in late-night classes. There were even lessons on how to skin and preserve roadkill for the tying bench. And Super Fly created innovative fly patterns like the shit fly and the fly line damsel. Many a fish was caught and released thanks to the conservation efforts encouraged by the shop.

Nobody really knows what happened to Super Fly. He started resembling the flies he tied, with feathers stuck in his beard and fur sprouting over his body. A month after his disappearance, I arrived and found the back door of the shop unlocked. Mercifully, the shop's contents were unmolested. There was a dire atmosphere, and the discovery of the carcass of a large coyote in the freezer added to the dark mystery. Had Super Fly regressed that far? Bill collectors, sheriff's deputies, and Super Fly's "fishing associates" from Española prowled the area. But he was nowhere to be found. So the flies and gear were sold off, the cases dispersed, and the page closed on the legendary first full fly shop of Taos.

But the sign of the six-foot rainbow was stuck away in storage in case it should be called upon for service. And sure enough, here comes Poundmeister Junior, Nick Streit, and his fiancée, Christina, both of clear head and heart—and with great résumés in the fly-fishing business. The new Taos Fly Shop started on the lean side, but there won't be any dead varmints in the freezer or fur flying through the air. The latest in flies and gear is on display, along with flies like the badger and double hackle that have worked for decades on the Rio. It is also the home of Streit Fly-fishing, where you can book guided trips in New Mexico, Colorado, or Argentina.

CHAPTER TWENTY-NINE

SUPER FLY SIGHTING

by Warren Dean McClenagan

■ ■ ■

I have excellent guides working for me and they take most of the trips into the rugged Rio. But after meeting Warren and his partner, Barry, I knew that I had found the raw farm boy talent that would draw Super Fly out into the light of day. So I decided to take them fishing myself. And as I correctly surmised, Warren had the literary skills necessary to accurately report any encounter with Super Fly—be it by choice or chance.

On that fateful day, so as not to alarm the old rapscallion—who is still into me for financial, physical, and physiological debts—I purposely started on the long hike out of the canyon well ahead of my anglers. Little did I suspect that SF would virtually accost the boys with his brand of jocularity.

—Taylor Streit

Trips to the Rio Grande in Northern New Mexico, for the fly fisherman, are never uneventful and rarely without incident of one kind or another that may or may not involve fish. Given my experience, I thought little of it when, on this year's trip, I encountered a character I might have thought odd were I not in the rarefied cultural atmosphere that typifies Taos, New Mexico. Indeed, I might never have given this fellow a second thought had my cousin and fishing buddy, Barry, not stumbled across an article from the *Horse Fly* a few days after our return. Titled "The Legend of Super Fly" and dated June 15, 2004, it described a local fly shop proprietor who cut a swath of

Elmer Guerri inducts Taylor Streit into the Freshwater Fishing Hall of Fame.

mythical proportions through the Taos fly-fishing community back in the 1980s only to disappear mysteriously and without a trace, save a few animal pelts and a coyote carcass, leftovers from his fly-tying enterprises.

After we read the article, there was no doubt in our minds that this was the self-same fellow we had crossed paths with one evening as we trudged out of the Rio Grande Gorge north of Questa. Granted, we came away with scant evidence. I only ask that "fly-fishing groupies" and "thugs" who had the dubious privilege of spending time with Super Fly during his brief but storied career in Taos, and have long wondered what became of him, will give me a hearing. Draw your own conclusion, but I, for one, believe that Super Fly may yet ride the currents of the Big River.

It had been another eventful day on the Rio Grande, chock-full of incidents, some of which even involved fish. What made the day different from numerous other assaults we have made on this river was the company we kept. Having enjoyed dabbling around in the side currents of fly-fishing for some years, we had determined that it was time to take it to the next level—that is, from fishing to catching fish. In order to make this leap, we hired renowned Freshwater-fishing Hall of Fame guide Taylor Streit of Taos. Coincidently, Mr. Streit happens to be the resident expert on the lore of Super Fly and the author of the aforementioned article. He also has, among other distinctions, that of being the very same Taylor Streit who followed in the footsteps of Super Fly himself in terms of being able to put fishermen together with fish. At the same time, Mr. Streit displays an unwavering sense of professionalism and dependability, the lack of which may well have driven the legendary Super Fly underground and out of business almost twenty years ago.

Barry and I are self-taught, having accumulated what we know of fly-fishing by trial and error; many trials and a lifetime of errors. Indeed one might say that we have learned virtually everything there is to know about not catching fish with a fly rod and have become quite proficient at it. We are further shackled by the kind of armchair education that results from living too far from the trout. We are thus forced to fish vicariously through the "success stories" of others whose accumulated advice leaves us fishing, most often, in the state of confusion. Suffice it to say that our bad habits were many and firmly ingrained. We knew we would need at least two days in the company of a master like Taylor to even begin to get the hang of catching a few of the fish we had been consistently spooking for years.

Careful consideration had gone into the choice of this particular guide. We had worn out several copies of Taylor's *No-Nonsense Guide to Fly Fishing New Mexico* over the years and recently devoured his latest publication, *Instinctive Fly Fishing*. I am not ashamed to admit that I have a tasteful shrine dedicated to the man in my den. We were on our second outing, already full to the brim with incidents, when we had our encounter—one, I feel safe in saying, many in the Taos area would consider on par with a sighting of Nessie or Sasquatch.

That day dawned cool and rainy—the effects of the edge of a Pacific hurricane, Taylor told us as he surveyed the water from the rim of the gorge high above the Rio

Grande. It did not bode well for fishing, and for the first time there was a glimmer of doubt in the guide's otherwise unflappable and infectious optimism. He recovered quickly: "But, if we are not going to catch fish, we might as well not be catching big ones!" he said. We spent the day scouring the seams, chutes, and eddies that form as the water pours around the huge basalt boulders that characterize this stretch of the river. Barry and I were elated at our success. Putting to use what Taylor, ever the professional, had taught us on a tamer stretch of the river the day before, we caught more trout in those few hours than we had ever caught on this river before, in all our many trips put together! But, despite our experience, the final analysis by the man was, "She's off today, boys. Big rivers can be that way." We shuddered to think what she might be like when she was "on."

The trip out is a grueling mile-long trail of switchbacks that snakes up the eastern wall of the gorge. It's a daunting trek even if you have not been stumbling upriver against a relentless current all day. As Barry and I stared at our respective piles of gear, trying to remember the arrangement that had allowed us to carry all that stuff down there, our guide made quick work of his scant belongings. The scene revealed, in stark relief, that where Taylor is "no-nonsense," Barry and I tended to be "mostly nonsense." I was trying to find a place for my portable grill and a two-pound sack of catfish bait (you never know) when Taylor, always alert for a teaching moment, reminded us that amateurs can be identified by two things they always bring to the river: too much crap and a poor casting stroke.

"I'm fifty-eight and I smoked for twenty years," he said, "so I'll start on up. I'm sure you guys will catch up with me." I suppose it took us another twenty or thirty minutes to get everything situated. Dusk was upon us by the time we began plodding up the trail.

Looking back, there was a mystical quality to the evening that foreshadowed what was to come. Another thunderstorm was moving in. The lightning was getting closer, ricocheting off the rim of the gorge and lighting up the sky, close enough to make us jump and duck instinctively at times. The gorge is not a safe place to be under these conditions, yet we were giddy with joy, reflecting on what we had learned and the fish we had caught. We were a little over halfway up when we heard an odd, birdlike call from the trail ahead. "That's what an osprey says when he is being chased by a bald eagle," we heard someone explain. Our first thought was that our guide had partaken of some sort of refreshment in our absence, but we quickly dismissed the idea. He was all business, that man. When we reached the next switchback we found the source of the call: a figure on his knees gathering little dark pods quicker than a squirrel in November. We looked at one another, bewildered.

"Ripe piñon nuts," said the mystery man. "These are delicious!"

I popped one in my mouth and crunched down just before he explained how to shell them. Embarrassed, I tried to spit out the hulls discretely.

"So you eat them like a sunflower seed?" Barry responded.

"No. Like a piñon nut," said the man, in a rather condescending tone. "I hope you know the difference in piñon nuts and deer droppings."

It has been a long time since anyone has laid eyes on Super Fly, and physical descriptions are sketchy at best. The last report was that, by the time of his disappearance, he was beginning to resemble the flies he tied. But such a description leaves much room for interpretation. Would that be the famed poundmeister, or the shit fly? I could not be certain, but I thought I saw a twig of wild watercress hanging in what was either a beard or a wad of dubbing material on his chin. Furthermore, the animal pelt, perhaps badger, dangling from the top of his pack, flapping in the breeze, created the impression that he might be some sort of superhero of angling. By then it was too dark to make out many features, and the lightning flashes and lack of oxygen working together might have made our minds play tricks on us. But in hindsight, judging by his behavior, we can think of no other explanation but that we had stumbled upon Super Fly himself!

"You guys have any luck?" he asked with a wily grin that seemed to indicate that he often used this question as a form of torture on those who were climbing out of the gorge.

"As a matter of fact, we did," I responded, "best day we have ever had on this river!"

"Warren caught a really nice rainbow on a little shit fly," Barry offered.

Those last two words clearly caught the piñon-nutter off guard. He paused for a moment and peered out over the gorge with a faraway look in his eye, like someone who has just heard the name of one of his children that he had not seen in years.

"Shit fly, huh." he said. "Folks still using that one?"

He seemed to be directing the question more to the river than to us. A bolt of lightning brought him out of his daze. The mystery man stood and plunged his hand into the pocket of his jacket.

"Next time, try one of these," he offered, pulling a small multicompartmented box from the recesses. He fingered around for a moment, mumbling something about deteriorating vision, and finally produced a small fly, which he handed to me.

"What is it?" I asked. He hesitated, as if the question were out of left field. Somewhere along the way, this mysterious fellow's fishing sense had evolved to a point where fly names were superfluous to him.

"I don't know," he said gruffly. "Fish don't eat names. Call it the 'no shit' fly. What does it matter?"

He stepped closer and took on a serious tone that reminded us a little of Taylor. I thought I detected a hint of head cement lacquer on his breath as he added, "When you tie this fly on . . ." He paused and looked over his shoulder like he was afraid someone might be eavesdropping. "When you tie this on, be sure to use an 'I shit you knot.'" He held his composure just long enough for the pun to sink in, then threw his head back and laughed until we feared he might topple off the trail.

At that moment, a bolt of lightning lit up the trail. "What the hell is that?" cried our companion, looking up over my shoulder. Startled, I braced myself, thinking perhaps he had seen a mountain lion poised to pounce from one of the boulders hanging over the trail. As it turns out, the poor fellow had gotten his first good look at Barry's backpack silhouetted against the storm-lit sky.

This beast was a relic of a bygone era when comfort and camping were considered mutually exclusive. Any sense of ergonomics had been sacrificed in favor of carrying capacity, which was roughly that of a typical subcompact car. Barry felt obligated to make the most of every cubic foot. The problem was compounded by the fact that Barry, a builder by trade, stores his backpack in the same garage as his construction tools. The two pursuits invariably spill over into one another so that he can frame while fishing or fish while framing if the mood strikes. I don't complain, mind you. Chalk line can make decent fly line backing in a pinch. His rod case, which contained the unbroken half of every rod he has ever owned, was attached to the back of the pack with bungee cords and swayed some three feet above his six-foot-four-inch frame. I suppose it was quite a sight, but I was used to it. In fact, it was a drastic improvement over some of the other traveling rigs he had carried. I once rescued him from certain death as he hung from a spruce, suspended by jumper cables he had used to secure his waders for the hike in.

"What the hell do you have in there?" the mysterious fellow asked, shaking his head incredulously.

"Most of the travel trailer," Barry responded without a hitch. "I thought I might want to frame up a bungalow while we were down there."

"You ain't developers, are ya?" the stranger growled. His eyes narrowed and flashed, like Clint Eastwood in *The Outlaw Josey Wales.*

"No, no!" Barry said, taking a step back. "We're just good ole boys out fly-fishing."

"Good," he said, looking us up and down. "Developers that wander off down in here have been known to . . . well, have accidents," he added, tapping the cork handle of the fly rod he carried at his side.

I felt, at this point, that it was in our best interest to return to the subject of fishing. Query revealed that this character, whatever else he might have been, had done some guiding himself. While Taylor had been extremely tactful about discussing his clientele, in keeping with his impeccable professional demeanor, this caped stranger was not above entertaining us with stories of "stupid" things "tough" clients had done on trips to the river. From there, he launched, with hardly a breath, into a tale about running short of goose biots for a particular fly pattern. And how, during the spontaneous hunt that followed, he dropped a goose that was flying out over a remote section of the gorge and was forced to follow a deer trail to the bottom to recover the bird. By the time he made it to the river, I understood him to say, he was riding the deer, which somehow seemed believable coming from him. Anyway, he claimed that he came out of the gorge with enough goose biots and deer hair to keep himself gainfully employed at the tying bench through the winter.

Changing subjects on a dime yet again, he recovered a serious tone and asked if we wanted to see something really cool. Our moms had taught us to run away in response to such questions, and I noticed that Barry was reaching for his framing hammer. The stranger produced a lighter, almost magically, from his vest. He struck it and held it up to one of the massive rocks that formed the upper wall of the trail.

"Look at that!" he said in a tone that seemed rustically reverent.

As we stepped in, we could see the light was dancing off an image drawn onto the boulder.

"Look at the proportions . . . the detail . . . the way the horns divide . . . The bounding gait . . . a mule deer, not a whitetail . . . and you know the difference, don't you . . ." He

Mule deer in the Rio Grande Gorge

was talking, not to us, but to the artist, as if honoring, even communing, somehow, over time, with a prehistoric companion who had stopped long enough to hallow this spot. I felt a sense of privilege wash over me. We were blessed to be here, now. Blessed to be here with someone who was still connected to the earth in a way that most of us no longer are. Blessed to be.

A crack of lightning brought us back to the present, reminding us that we must move on. "We'd better get going," I said.

"Where?" he asked innocently.

"To the trailhead." The idea seemed to bewilder him, so I explained, "To our truck. Are you going that way?"

"Now why would I want to do that?" he asked, in a way that made me feel stupid for asking.

It was beginning to rain, so we left the fellow there. The last we saw of him, he was sipping rainwater out of a pocket in a boulder, and humming—a Coltrane tune, I think it was. He seemed oblivious to the rain that beaded up and slid off of him as if he exuded some sort of bio-floatant. Obviously he was in his element and could take care of himself. When we met Taylor at the top, we were eager to ask whether he had come across the stranger. Alas, the rain cut loose and we were forced to toss our gear in and retreat to our respective vehicles for protection. It was dark as our guide led us back toward civilization, and somewhere near Questa, he slipped out of sight into the rainy night.

Super Fly being beamed up.

Would that I had even a grainy snapshot to validate my story; but, alas, my camera was buried in my pack, between my battery-powered socks and my coffee grinder. The only evidence I carried away was the fly this stranger gave me. I would describe it this way. It resembles a bead head hare's ear bereft of tail, hackle, and rib, much like the shit fly. But it has also been plucked clean of its dubbing, leaving only a small mound of black thread, unwinding, and the bead, which slides halfway up and down the hook shank. The next time I am in Taos, I will loan it to Taylor for forensic analysis, and this mystery can be laid to rest. Until then, keep the sun at your back and your fly in the water, and, if you are fortunate, and if he's in the mood, you may just stumble upon Super Fly, caped crusader of the gorge.

CHAPTER THIRTY

THE LEGEND OF SPIFMEISTER

■ ■ ■

Most people are introduced to fishing casually. Perhaps on a Sunday afternoon, after eating some hot dogs at a cookout, little Jimmy is plopped on the bank and handed a Snoopy rod. The easy pastime takes or it doesn't—with the outcome perhaps dependent on the fish's appetite. On occasion, the little fisher gets fascinated by the ancient game and is hooked for life.

But poor baby Nick Streit didn't have any choice in the matter. Born the son of a fly-fishing guide, his birth was prematurely induced by a turbulent four-wheel-drive ride up to a remote lake. It would be nice to say that he was raised on purpose to follow in his father's profession, like the son of a European craftsman, but his dad is a Taoseño and lacks such foresight. Still, since Nick was often found streamside, he got tutored in fly-fishing by his dad.

Nick's first fly rod was built especially for his size; the thing wasn't four feet long. He started to get in lots of time on—and in—the water, as his preference was to act like a fish rather than to try and catch one. He'd try to accommodate his dad by pretending to fish, but he couldn't resist the allure of the water, and before long he'd purposely step on the slickest boulder he could find and slide down into the river. Then, when his old man would instruct him to get out, he'd exit on the same slick rock so that he could be assured of going for another ride into the drink.

But an event happened when he was about six years old that got him more interested in learning to cast and fish. Dad took him to the Rio Grande and ran into a friend named Duane Maktima. He was there with his son Norm. As previously mentioned, Nick preferred swimming over fishing, but little Norm was the same age as Nick and outcast him badly. That incident seemed to inspire Nick, and by

Nick with a freshwater brown trout in Argentina. Photo by Gabe Fontanazza

the time he was twelve, world-famous casting coach Mel Krieger even compli-
mented him on his tight loops.

Toughening Up

But Nick's serious fishing education started when he was thirteen. Dad was trying to set
up a bonefishing business in the Bahamas and Nick went with him for the winter. Nick's
folks had been apart for some time and he had been living with Mom. She knew that
he was pretty soft, and he was to be taken away and "toughened up," as she tearfully put
it. South Andros Island couldn't be a better place, as it's not the Bahamas most people
think of, with cruise ships and idle beach lounging. No, this was one of the remote "family islands," and the islanders' black skin was untainted with white blood.

A very foreign country for a spongy boy, but Nick volunteered for a semester of
school there. He was easy to find in the after-school crowd because he was the only
white child there. He was indeed an oddity and tried to bolster himself up by being

cool. He had bestowed upon himself the handle of "Spifmeister," but nobody had any idea what that meant, and the closest translation in Bahamian was "Spitmeister." This fit, because like most young toughs he was fond of the manly art of spittin'—young Nick couldn't take three steps without hurling a luggie. Despite this dubious title, the white boy quickly became popular and was even cheered when he kicked the school bully's ass. The kid bopped Nick on the head with a Vitamalt bottle, but that was not a serious deterrent for a Streit's thick skull. The principal witnessed the battle and extended Nick hearty congratulations, while the bully got a "proper caning."

Nick's other toughening-up experiences included a middle-of-the-night encounter with a six-foot python. It was about midnight at a remote beach house in the Caribbean jungle. We were sleeping off a long day of spear fishing; I was snoozing upstairs and Nick downstairs. A flurry of moaning and mumbling awakened me. I called down and asked him what was wrong. He said in an unconscious monotone, "I can't get the fish off my spear." I said, "You're just dreaming, go back to sleep." A few minutes later I was again awakened by more moaning from below. This was soon replaced—as a light was switched on—by exceptionally loud screaming. I jumped out of bed and flew down the stairs to witness my twelve-year-old son flying about the room, hollering like a monkey, with a six-foot snake wrapped around his arm! (The light that Nick had to turn on was a bare bulb that had to be screwed in by raising both arms up; his first sight of the snake had been only inches away from his eyes.) To spice up the event even further, he smashed his elbow while doing his snake dance and was bleeding on the snake.

I'm glad that I'm getting to tell you this story before my son does, because our memories differ on the next part. I recall jumping into the fray with manly authority and unwrapping the six-foot-long serpent from his arm. His version is that I yelled instructions concerning the constrictor removal from the other side of the room. In either event the squirmy bastard was soon a headless squirmy bastard. But Nick was in bad shape and had been slimed by the reptile; an unbelievably foul green substance covered his arm. We scrubbed it off the best we could, but Nick was in shock and hysterical about the snake's whereabouts; all night he shook and asked, "Is it gone? Is it dead?"

This put the Spifmeister in a state of shock for a day, but it was a small price to pay for the esteem he garnered as the story quickly spread from Deep Creek to Kemps Bay. Most people speculated that they would have been dead from fright as a result of such an encounter. But others were envious, and one dopey kid, who was Nick's rival in the neighborhood, boasted that it had also happened to him. But he made the boast several days after the event, and he said it had happened years before but he had "never bothered to tell anybody."

Perhaps the toughest part of Nick's toughening up was simply living on this wild beach alone with Dad. All parents know about the test of wills that constantly occurs with their kids, but here it was intensified because there were few distractions: no TV, no electricity, no place to go, and no way to get there. And most of all, no Mom around to clean up—just grumpy Dad with his firm commitment to do no more than fifty percent of the chores. This caused a great deal of friction, and sparks flew everywhere. The old man was pretty abrasive to start with, having failed in the bonefishing venture and being reduced to tying flies to get by. And if things weren't tense enough, Dad's long-distance girlfriend would visit once a month from Houston to insane-a-tize the island. (Nick's father felt guilty for years afterward over all the grief he gave the boy. Dad only recently realized that even though he didn't have very subtle parenting skills at the time, the battle of wills sorely needed to be won by Father.)

Hula Dancing with Sharks

Dad and Nick took extended camping trips to the southern end of Andros Island—a remote place, hard to reach except by means of little flats boats. Several miles of open ocean had to be crossed. Weighed down by fifty-five-gallon drums of water and fuel, the boat would wallow around in the big waves. When they finally arrived at the south end of the island, all senses remained on high alert, because the next human was thirty-five miles away, and the price of being careless could be your life. Something as simple as getting cut could kill you.

Fortunately, there were no serious mishaps, but there were some interesting fishing tales. One of these occurred when Nick was trow-lining ("throw" in English but "trow" in Bahamian). He was in the skiff catching gray snapper, but he kept getting ripped off by a giant 'cuda. Spifmeister tied a separate rig for the 'cuda with wire and a big hunk of snapper. He tossed it off to the side and kept track of it by tying it to his waist because he wanted to continue fishing for snapper. Presently, a shark happened by and ate the snapper bait. As Nick turned around to fight it, Mr. Bari' took off running on the other line. This spun Nick around and wrapped the shark line around him. He was nearly flipped into the water as the two nastiest varmints in the sea pulled on him from port and starboard. Although he landed the shark, the 'cuda line fortunately parted from his waist. Nick's sensitive and overprotective father fortunately missed this hula act as he was off fishing for bonefish on a nearby flat.

Nick learned a lot about fishing with trow line and spear. When you're hungry and fishing for sustenance, the lessons learned are driven home with more meaning than when practicing silly catch-and-release fishing. The only food at the one store was canned and expensive, and the boys needed protein badly. They lived on a big expanse of shallow water and at low tide it was possible to walk out into the sea for a mile. Nick would go out to fetch supper and Pop would watch him with binoculars so he would know when to get the pan hot. It was possible to tell what was on the menu by observing the boy's actions: if he reached downward a few times the cook's mouth would start to water, because Nick mostly likely had come across conch. If he had the fly rod, and was fishing close, he was after box fish.

But as the boy had inherited some serious fish karma, Dad kept the glasses on him out of his previously declared parental concern, too. And one time when he was watching Nick through the glasses, the boy started hopping around and slashing his fly rod about as if he were fencing with some underwater adversary. Then he turned tail and appeared to run across the surface of the water. When he got home, the fly rod was much shorter than when he left, as the result of a duel with a shark. Having fish karma is . . . maybe good . . . maybe bad, and can mean that one of the Streits will someday be eaten by a fish.

Hauled Downriver by a Rainbow

Nick came away from the island a lean young man, citizen of the world, and ready to take on new challenges. He made it through the rugged Taos, New Mexico, school system without any permanent damage. And at seventeen he was on the United States Junior Fly Fishing Team. Out of more than one hundred applicants, six kids were chosen to represent the United States. A couple were from Colorado and another was from New Mexico. That was Norm Maktima, the kid on the Rio Grande whose good casting so many years before had goaded Nick into becoming a fine caster himself.

Young Nick gets the day off from school in the Bahamas, circa 1993.

Nick and Norm took off for the Colorado practices in Nick's old jeep. They were low on food but nabbed a rabbit that happened too close to the country boys. After throwing rocks at the stationary rabbit, they saw their chance at a good dinner hopping away, but Norm launched a last rock, and by leading the critter ten feet, conked it on the head.

The team practiced in several locales in the United States, and got special instruction on fishing UK lakes by Welshman Dave Wooten. In Wales, they met kids from all over the world. They were fishing for trout and grayling, and the U.S. team surprised everyone by coming in second after the Czech Republic. "The lake fishing was very different than the way we fish lakes in the States," Nick said. "You cast ahead of the drifting boat and retrieve the flies back to you. Thanks to the training I got from Davy Wooten and Duane Hada, I was able to catch a very good fish in the reservoir." Norm got into some rising grayling, figured them out, and won the individual title. The boys got their pictures on the covers of magazines, were TV celebrities, and received loads of free gear from fly-fishing manufacturers.

"That opened my eyes to a bigger world of fishing and got me serious about fly-fishing," he said. "And when I got back, I started taking guide trips out on my own. It was great being my own boss at seventeen. I had apprenticed with my dad for several years, carrying lunches, gear, and even a baby on one trip. And, of course, I had been fishing with him a lot, but I never paid much attention to him, as he was forever telling me this and that. But I soon discovered that the stuff my dad had been teaching me was actually true."

Nick has since run jet boats in Alaska and guided in Argentina. But when asked about his favorite place to fish, he says:

> The Rio Grande is just minutes from my front door and is still one of the most fantastic rivers anywhere—just being in that canyon is pretty amazing, let alone while being hauled downriver by a powerful rainbow. Just the other day my dad and I went and he hooked a three-pounder that ran between a narrow hole in some rocks. He had to pass his rod through the hole and when it came out the other side the rod started drifting down the rapids. He splashed after it and when he caught up with it he reeled up, and the big fish

was still attached. The exact thing happened to me a few minutes later—exact except my fish was bigger.

When asked if he plans to stay in the fishing racket, Nick says:

I have worked in several fly shops, so it was just a natural progression for my fiancée, Chrissy, and I to reopen my dad's old Taos Fly Shop. It's nice to have a place where I can control the atmosphere and talk fishing. Local folks can come in and ask any kind of fishing question and not feel intimidated, because I grew up fishing here and went through the same process. My dad closed the shop when I was only seven, but I have all these memories of being here as a little kid and it sure feels right to be here now. ■